CONQUEST AND CAPITALISM

1492 - 1992

written and illustrated by Steve Brouwer

Big Picture Books
PO Box 909, Carlisle, PA 17013
717-249-2763

TABLE OF CONTENTS

Part I

Chapter 1

COLUMBUS AND THE CAPITALIST CONQUEST: 1492–1992

We know, by reading from Columbus' diary, what motivated him to sail across the Atlantic:

> *"One who has gold does as he wills in the world, and it even sends more souls to heaven."*

And, that he thought he had God's blessing to collect humans for profit as well as gold:

> *"Let us in the name of the Holy Trinity go on sending all the slaves that can be sold."*

There was never any question in his mind that he could force the people of America to work for the profit of Europe:

> *"On my arrival in the Indies, I took by force, in the first island I found, some of these natives that they might learn our language and give me information."*

> *"The Indians... are naked and defenseless, hence ready to be given orders and put to work."*

Three years after his arrival in America in 1492, Columbus began establishing a number of systems for extracting the wealth of the New World. In his new colony on the island of Hispaniola, each male Indian was ordered to deliver a small flask filled with gold every three months.

Those who failed had their hands chopped off.

COLUMBUS AND THE CAPITALIST CONQUEST: 1492-1992

Five centuries ago Christopher Columbus sailed the Ocean Sea, searched for the riches of the Indies, and accidentally bumped into America. When many people in Europe and America celebrate the 500th anniversary of his daring voyage to the New World, they are applauding the heroic effort of the navigator, the spread of Christianity to the new continents, and the ascendence of European culture. More than anything, however, they are cheering the triumph of capitalism.

When we celebrate Columbus, we are, either consciously or unconsciously, glorifying the exploits of those who go out into the world and do whatever it takes to bring home the profits.

The original profitable activity, "the primitive accumulation of capital," was the actual seizure and forced extraction of wealth from America. This kind of capitalism arrived in America with Christopher Columbus and allowed him to begin the cruel and unrelenting process which would transport extraordinary wealth to Europe, thereby elevating it (and later the United States) to uncontested prominence in the world. Columbus and the Europeans who followed him enslaved and exterminated the indigenous people of America, expropriated virtually all their lands and treasures, and imported many millions of African slaves to extract the wealth from the New World's plantations and mines.

This process of forced extraction accumulated the wealth necessary for the industrial revolution and for the technologically sophisticated production of manufactured goods which we now associate with capitalism. And although slavery no longer exists, in many places the modern sector of industrial capitalism still depends on the coercion and exploitation of labor for its profitability. Also, of course, forms of primitive accumulation of capital still exist today in various parts of the globe, brutalizing the local inhabitants while often earning the highest returns for the investor in Europe, the United States, and Japan (for examples, we need only look to the plantations of El Salvador; the gold and diamond mines of South Africa, and the sugar fields of the Philippines.)

Columbus and most of the adventurers who followed him were driven by an insatiable desire to get rich quickly and by the firmly implanted faith that they were blessed by God in all their endeavors. Columbus' own thoughts, as quoted above from his notebooks, express his motivations very well: he wanted to find gold and other riches, enslave the inhabitants of America whenever it seemed propitious, and save their souls on behalf of Christianity. In such endeavors he and the other Europeans who followed in his footsteps were certain that God was on their side and would help them accomplish anything. Columbus wrote:

> "Thus the eternal God, our Lord, gives victory over apparent impossibilities to those who follow in his way."

Because he was well-armed with such certainty, Columbus wasted no time when he landed on the tiny Caribbean island of Guanahani on October 12, 1492. Although he was met by friendly, gentle people who marveled at his ships, he immediately took prisoners because he was convinced they could lead him to the fabled gold mines of the East. There was, in reality, little gold in the Caribbean, but Columbus and the Spanish colonists had an insatiable passion for wealth. Within fifty years, their efforts to ferret out every last gold nugget had led to the extermination of almost all the original Americans who inhabited the West Indies.

THE REALITY OF AMERICA

This is a harsh depiction of Columbus, but a true one, and it represents a necessary counterpoint to the fairy tale stories which North Americans have heard since earliest childhood. These glossy enhancements of reality include not only the Columbus stories, but the various Horatio Alger and Chamber of Commerce versions of economic growth and development in America which omit the cruelties that often accompany capitalist success. The driving spirit behind the conquest of America was nicely summed up by Adam Smith under the heading:

> "the Motives for Establishing new Colonies"
>
> Columbus turned his view towards their minerals; and in the richness of the production... he found full compensation... As a result of the representations of Columbus, the Council of Castile determined to take possession of the countries in which the inhabitants were plainly incapable of defending themselves. The pious purpose of converting them to Christianity sanctified the injustice of the project. But the hope of finding treasures of gold there was the sole motive which prompted them to undertake it.
> -from The Wealth of Nations, 1776

If Smith, the prophet of capitalism, was able to clearly describe the motivation of Columbus and his followers, then it was Karl Marx, the prophet of socialism, who explained what this kind of activity meant for the development of capitalism:

The discovery of gold and silver in America, the extirpation, enslavement, and entombment in mines of the aboriginal population, the beginning of the conquest and looting of the East Indies, the turning of Africa into a warren for the commercial hunting of black-skins, signalized the rosy dawn of the era of capitalist production. These idyllic proceedings are the chief momenta of primitive accumulation.
                                        -from *Capital, volume III*

Marx produced his appraisal of the dawn of capitalism at the same moment that triumphant capitalist society elevated Columbus to the status of archetypal hero at the end of the nineteenth century. His voyage was an important symbol for the new capitalist class in America, the so-called "robber barons" who wanted to justify their own aggressive drive for wealth. They admired Columbus' "entrepreneurial spirit" because he was the particular kind of adventurer who risked all to become rich and famous; and, even more important, he enriched many times over the venture capitalists who backed him. When the United States elevated Columbus to his grand place in history in 1892 and celebrated the 400th anniversary of his voyage by staging the great Columbian Exposition, it was poised to become a great world power. The United States, like Columbus, felt that Divine Providence was sending it forth to make its way in the world.

Whatever the reasons that Columbus reached heroic proportions, however, our purpose is not to pretend that he was the consummate villain or the incarnation of evil. Let us give Columbus his due as a courageous navigator who was doggedly determined to succeed on his voyage. Columbus was neither unusually good or bad, but was typical of the Europeans of his age in many ways; those who followed him were often more ruthless than he was, and only occasionally more cognizant of the destruction they brought to the Americas.

Likewise we should not claim that America was an earthly paradise inhabited by pure and innocent souls before the Europeans arrived. We know that the Aztec and Inca civilizations in Mexico and Peru ruled over well-regulated and prosperous agricultural economies governed by harsh monarchies which could match the cruelty and bloodthirstiness of many Old World societies. Yet compared to the old regimes in both the Old World and the New World, the conquest of America was something quite distinct. It announced to the world that the exploitation of human life would proceed on a whole new scale: an astonishing num-ber of people, continents full of people - not just in America, but in Africa and Asia as well - would have to sink to new levels of subjugation and degradation in order to lift up the fortunes of the Europeans. Nor would this process be intermittent like the depredations so often endured by societies from ancient times: it did not resemble the occasional looting of defenseless populations by roving hordes of barbarians or the murderous punishments meted out by mad kings. The new system begun in America would expand into a sustained economic mechanism which would span the globe and steadily suck up the world's riches for centuries.

THE STRUCTURE OF ECONOMIC AND SOCIAL DOMINATION

These systematic mechanisms of capitalism are not associated with Christopher Columbus simply because he was the first on the scene in America, nor because he has been chosen as the mythic hero of the Christian European triumph. A more important consideration is that the methods and rationale for the exploitation of the New World were introduced very quickly in the Caribbean by Columbus and his immediate successors. Eight characteristics which describe how this form of economic domination worked, and still works, can be listed as follows:

1. Investment capital was put forward by the very rich - the monarchs, the bankers, and the wealthy merchants.

2. This capital funded expeditions and enterprises designed by entrepreneurs and conquistadors; they would extract the wealth of the New World by any means necessary.

3. Vast profits were realized - the larger portion generally went to the capitalists calmly waiting for their ships to come in; a few of the most ruthless and successful entrepreneurs became capitalists themselves.

4. In order to enforce this process of accumulation, extreme amounts of organized violence were required - millions of people had to be coerced into working.

5. In order to justify the inhuman treatment and subjugation of other humans, a racist ideology which denied their humanity had to be developed.

6. In order to keep these oppressed people from rebelling successfully, local elites, usually colonial or neo-colonial white people, had to align themselves with the military and capital forces of Europe (and later the United States.)

7. This 500 year old system almost always needed religious justification - God's name had to be invoked in order to legitimize or cover up the extensive racism and brutality, and to celebrate the acquisitive spirit and the cultural superiority of the invaders.

8. Finally, in most parts of the New World, the extraction of profits through mining, agriculture, and lumbering was accomplished in the quickest way possible; not only was human life sacrificed readily, but there also was little thought for the careful cultivation and maintenance of resources and land. When precious metals petered out or the soil was completely wasted, very poor people were left behind to scratch the earth's crust for survival. Meanwhile capital marched on in search of fresh bounty.

This eight part process of domination helped accumulate the capital that filled up the treasure houses of Europe and was later sufficient to form the base of the industrial revolution and usher in the era of industrial capitalism in Europe and the United States. The early kinds of capitalism, that extracted mineral wealth from far away mountain ranges and agricultural riches from vast systems of plantations, were nonetheless ventures devised to pay back investors with a healthy profit on their shares. These "primitive" capitalist activities have not disappeared today; they still represent a major kind of economic activity in many American, Asian, and African countries and even in some parts of the United States itself.

This book is not written to denigrate Columbus nor to convince the reader that 500 years ago the Europeans who ventured to America were a mean and brutal bunch. The real point is that a destructive system of exploitation still exists throughout much of our hemisphere, in fact, throughout most of the world. Not only do peasants in Central America struggle against overwhelming odds to throw off the old plantation system, but most countries of our hemisphere are trying to escape from the incredible weight of international debt which their military leaders and local capitalists have contracted with the bankers of the industrialized world. As 1992 arrives, almost all of Latin America and the Caribbean have suffered through more than a decade of economic depression and misery; living standards have fallen and sickness and poverty afflict more children than ever. Such is the degree of economic malfunction that we can safely say that never before have so many Americans lived in such poor circumstances as they do today.

Many who live in the United States tend to think that America was blessed by a special connection to God and the spirit of capitalism. However, most Americans live outside of the United States and have never benefited from the powerful capitalist wind that blew Columbus across the Ocean to America. Latin America and the Caribbean have had a long history of suffering at each change in the course of capitalist development. Their accumulated misery has made them more familiar with the social and economic history of the New World, a history much lengthier than ours. Long before there were even the smallest permanent settlements of Europeans in North America, there were rich cities springing up throughout the rest of America: Mexico City, Lima, Guatemala City, San Juan, Rio de Janiero, Santo Domingo, and many other places were part of a vast network which exported wealth back to Europe in the 16th, 17th, and 18th centuries.

Thus we begin a discussion of conquest and capitalism by looking at the kind of colonization and business enterprise practiced by Columbus himself and the conquistadors who immediately followed him. Then, we turn attention to some of the notable trends that have characterized 500 years of capitalist development of the New World: mining by enslaved Americans in the 16th and 17th century; the great trade in African slaves and sugar; the modernization of the economies of Chile, Cuba, and Mexico in the 19th and 20th centuries; some glimpses of the industrial development of the U.S.A. and Brazil.

Through the course of examining such mercantilist and industrial development it is necessary to take an occasional look at the role which religion has played: first as the apologetic for slavery and inequality; also as the source of spirited, if usually unsuccessful, protest against injustice at various times over the past 500 years; finally as the battleground on which two contemporary forces, Christian fundamentalism and the theology of liberation, fight for moral authority. We examine how the forces of religion, political repression, and U.S. capitalist hegemony converge in the struggles throughout Central America.

In the final chapters of the book, we quickly consider the fact that the patterns of capitalist excess are not peculiar to the Americas. The trends that characterized the European conquest have evolved into a political economy, a world system, that has enveloped the globe. It is within this capitalist world system, with its divisions between North and South, between capital and labor, that we must look for solutions to our current dilemmas.

REFLECTING UPON 1992

The 500th anniversary of the European conquest does not merit an orgy of self-congratulation. Rather, we should mark the date as a crucial one for the future of all of the Americas, including the United States. In recent years, the U.S. has taken a downward slide; it failed to invest its financial capital wisely and to make provisions for the social well-being of its people, while it wasted trillions of dollars on ill-founded speculation and useless military hardware. More and more, because of its increased poverty and homelessness, as well as the difficulty in maintaining the standard of living of most working people, the United States is beginning to resemble the rest of America. Through a process of growing inequality, the U.S. is becoming "Latin Americanized."

The United States needs to recognize its fall from grace; despite its swaggering display of military superiority in the Persian Gulf, the U.S. has reached the limits of its imperial power. Europe and Japan now hold the bulk of economic might in the capitalist world. The Europeans may have more reason to celebrate the Conquest than Americans do, since the unification of the European Economic Community in 1992 creates the greatest capitalist market in the world. And Japan, which now has the ten or twelve largest banks in the world, has decisively replaced the U.S. as the major center of international finance and investment capital.

Since the United States now enjoys the dubious status of being the world's largest debtor nation, a large proportion of its working population faces the risk of joining the other countries in the hemisphere who are used and abused at the whim of international capital. The United States should not feel superior to the rest of the Americas, but instead should acknowledge its common past and its present cultural ties. Soon, probably within fifty years, the U.S. will resemble most of its neighbors; it will be a truly multi-racial country without a white majority.

Now is an appropriate time to reject the Columbus myth and its undertones of racist and nationalist superiority. The world production of goods and culture has become ever more integrated; the separations between North and South, between rich and poor, and between "white" and "colored" are more evident and frightening than ever. The legacy of exploitation and inequality is stamped into the character of world economic and political relationships. It seems no accident that while the economic fortunes of the white races of the North keep increasing at the expense of the misery of the rest of the world, that racism is reviving itself in the United States and growing steadily in Europe. The whole nature of world-wide production is changing rapidly, so that the workers of the South are not only producing raw materials for the corporations of the North, but also ever greater quantities of manufactured goods.

The second half of the industrial revolution is well under way; or putting it another way, the industrial plantations are now being set up alongside the agricultural plantations and the neo-colonial mines and oil fields. The majority of the world's working classes now live outside of the industrialized North and they are even more harshly exploited than the generations of men and women who suffered through the first Industrial Revolution in Europe and the United States.

As this process of reorganizing the whole world according to the principles of industrial capitalism takes place, there are a great many struggles taking place to determine whether the people themselves, the workers who produce the wealth, shall exercise some degree of democratic control over their lives. Some of the bitterest conflicts are in the Americas, but their counterparts are everywhere: in Africa, Asia, and Latin America the search for profit is accompanied by the need to severely discipline the people who produce the profits. There are political and religious ramifications of this disciplinary effort: semi-fascist regimes in the South have found eager backers and military suppliers in the North; economic experts from such organizations as the International Monetary Fund counsel debt-ridden countries to impose austerity on families who already do not have enough to eat; and new strains of fundamentalism are preaching against religious humanism and democratic socialism, while teaching obedience to economic and political authorities.

It is the unhappy task of this book to quickly review this grim record, past and present, and to show how a capitalist economy and culture have spread throughout the Americas and the entire world system. The immediate future does not promise much relief for the vast majority of humankind unless many people, working simultaneously in many parts of the world, are able to use principles of democracy and equality to impose constraints on capital. Let us hope that this process can be peaceful, that billions of world citizens can convince a tiny, but very powerful minority of the destructiveness and moral emptiness embodied in the sentiment that drove Columbus, and those who have followed him, relentlessly onward. For the world can no longer survive if it is governed by the golden rule of Christopher Columbus:

"One who has gold does as he wills in the world."

Chapter 2

ENTREPRENEUR SHIP

Columbus called his scheme:

The Enterprise of the Indies

The Venture Capitalists:	The Entrepreneur:
Queen Isabella & King Ferdinand	Christopher Columbus
Their share: 90% of the profits	His share: 10% of the profits
Other motivation: Christianize the heathen savages	Other motivation: The title "Admiral of the Ocean Sea"

The entrepreneur has to say whatever the investor wants to hear. Columbus told Isabella that the native Americans would be the happy, willing workers in his entrepreneurial scheme and would make ideal Christians when they were converted:

> *"They are a very loving race and without covetousness and suitable to any use and I declare to your Highnesses that there is no better country nor better people in the world. They love their neighbors as they do themselves and their speech is the softest in the world being always accompanied by smiles."*

6

ENTREPRENEUR SHIP

In the typical capitalist project or adventure, the entrepreneur must convince the rich venture capitalists that he can provide them with a very high return on their investment, a sum much greater than they could earn by lending it out or watching it gain interest in the bank. The entrepreneur organizes the whole profit-making scheme and prepares to manage the enterprise while the capitalists invest all or most of the money. Columbus spent years trying to convince the Spanish monarchs to pay for his voyages toward the West, which he was sure offered the fastest and easiest route to the riches of China and the East Indies. When he finally convinced them, he had to agree to their terms, 90% for those who put up the cash and only 10% for himself, the man who would risk his life sailing toward the edge of the world.

Columbus guessed that the earth was about 12,000 miles in circumference, which would make the distance from Spain to the Indies only about 2,000 miles. There were many other sailors and astronomers in Portugal and Europe who believed that the world was round, but most of them thought, correctly, that it was much larger than Columbus imagined and that he would have to sail 15,000 miles across the ocean vastness to reach the riches of the East. There were also tales of mysterious islands lying amidst the Ocean Sea, but no one knew that the two vast American continents blocked the way.

In any case, the crucial ingredient in Columbus' entreaties to Queen Isabella was not the precision of his calculations, but his profession of great Christian faith. She backed his voyage because of his certainty that God approved of his expedition, his determination to convert the heathens in the Indies to Catholicism, and his prediction that he would return with unbelievable riches. This new wealth, he said, would be available to the Spanish armies so they could resume the crusades against the Moslems and recapture Jerusalem.

In relation to the other events that aroused Isabella's tremendous religious passions in 1492, Columbus' voyage seemed like an insignificant side event. Earlier in the same year the Spanish had succeeded in driving the last of the Islamic infidels, the Moors, out of their kingdom of Granada in the south of Spain. Then, the Church and the monarchy, having begun the great persecution known as the Inquisition a few years earlier, decided that 1492 was the year to drive the Jews, or "Christ killers," out of Spain. Many of those Jews who did not escape were burned at the stake as heretics. The vibrant culture of Jews and Moors in Spain, which had kept learning and science alive for centuries, was violently attacked - thousands of books and learned studies were burned, all for the glory of God. Ironically, converted Jews were among the leading backers of Columbus' enterprise and helped persuade the Queen to launch his voyage.

Since Isabella was convinced after the religious victories in Spain that heathen souls must be harvested in other parts of the world, and because King Ferdinand reluctantly agreed that there was the chance of a windfall for the Spanish treasury, the monarchs were finally amenable to Columbus' arguments. Columbus, for his part, was perfectly sincere in professing his simultaneous love of God and his love of gold; he mused about his impending good fortune:

> *"One who has gold does as he wills in the world, and it even sends more souls to paradise."*

The conquistador, Hernando Cortez, who forty years later delivered extraordinary wealth to the Spanish crown when he looted and destroyed the Aztec civilization, described the lust for gold in different terms:

> *"We Spanish suffer from a sickness of the heart for which gold is the only cure."*

One did not have to be Spanish, or Italian like Columbus, to suffer from this disease. Gianni Granzotto, in his generally sympathetic biography of Columbus, described how Columbus developed his thirst for gold while accompanying the Portuguese on a business voyage to Africa:

> *"It was his voyage to Guinea that first awakened the attraction to gold that would obsess him for the rest of his life... this feverish desire... was offset in his own conscience - thus morally justified - by his exaltation of the Christian faith."*

> *"On the expedition to Guinea all the Portuguese ships flew banners of the Cross and preached of liberating the Holy Sepulchre from Mohammedan dominion by means of the gold found in Africa... the theme of recapturing Jerusalem with the gold discovered in the new lands would arise repeatedly during Columbus' Atlantic adventures."*

It was the Portuguese, not the Spanish nor the Italian mercenaries like Columbus and Amerigo Vespucci, who had initiated the European habit of voyaging the oceans and trafficking in gold. From the middle of the 15th century they had colonized the West coast of Africa, the "Gold Coast," built forts and extracted considerable amounts of gold. Since Columbus had married into a Portuguese merchant family and lived and worked in Portugal for years before he went to Spain, he learned of the profitable sugar plantations the Portuguese had set up in 1469 on Sao Tomas, an island off the coast of Guinea. These plantations, worked by African slaves, were to become the model for the slave economy that later transformed the Caribbean.

If Columbus had not sailed intrepidly toward the West, another brave European mariner would have discovered the Americas a few years later and brought the dominance of European imperialism with him. Most likely he, too, would have been fortified with a religious faith which bolstered his courage and justified his actions, and would have employed harsh measures to insure that the "enterprise" was successful. The lure of untold riches was irresistible to the sea-going Europeans; often it seemed to diminish their capacity for generosity, too.

THERE IS NO HONOR AMONG ENTREPRENEURS

Columbus was not a generous man. Rodrigo Triano, a common sailor on Columbus' first voyage, had first sighted land at 2 a.m. on the morning of October 12, 1492. His shipmates rushed on deck, confirmed his sighting, and congratulated him on winning the generous lifetime pension which the King of Spain had promised to the first man to spy land. Rodrigo never received the reward of 10,000 maravedis, however, because Columbus himself claimed he had seen a flicker of candle light on the land ahead the evening before. None of the sailors believed him because they knew they had been too far away the night before to glimpse even a large bonfire. But Columbus, as commander of the expedition, prevailed upon the Spanish Court to give the reward to him instead of Rodrigo.

Greed created conflict with other members of the expedition, too. Mario Alonzo Pinzon, Columbus' chief pilot and captain of the Pinta, had been recruited for the voyage along with his highly skilled brothers because of their navigating expertise. Pinzon claimed that he and his family had been promised a fifty-fifty split of Columbus' share of the profits. Columbus denied this and kept his whole share for himself. Columbus died a moderately wealthy man in 1506 at the age of 51; but in the years before his death he was deeply embittered because he felt certain that King Ferdinand had cheated him out of a much larger fortune. Thus, long after his death the Spanish courts were filled with petitions from both the families of Pinzon and Columbus, each claiming that it had lost its rightful share in the plunder of America.

SAINT CHRISTOPHER COLUMBUS?

This unhappy man did not gain his prominent place in history for three hundred years. The Vatican published "De Propaganda Fide" in 1622, which attempted to set a new religious agenda for the Americas and make some amends for the brutality of the conquest. In this document Columbus was named as "God's messenger," the one designated in the Great Plan of history to spread the word of the Bible to the New World. This effort did not succeed and the real exaltation of Columbus' deeds came in the 19th century, when various people found it propitious to revive his name. Washington Irving wrote a biography of him in 1825 and elevated him to the status of America's first hero. As the century wore on, the spirit of Columbus seemed to mesh with the brash, optimistic spirit of industrial capitalism, which was sure of the righteousness of its entrepreneurial instincts and also eager to export its ideas of progress and Christianity to other parts of the world. This culminated with the great Columbian Exposition of 1892 on the 400th anniversary of Columbus' voyage.

The Catholic Church nearly made Columbus a saint in time for the celebration. Pope Pius IX, who before he ascended to the papacy had traveled in the Americas and had been disappointed that so few monuments to Columbus existed, initiated beatification proceedings in 1866. The Church was interested in building up its legitimacy and fighting anti-Catholic prejudice in the United States, which was still under the sway of the Protestant majority even as it became home to more and more Catholic immigrants. The Vatican review of Columbus' life, however, found some things unacceptable in a saint. First, it could not be denied that Columbus had introduced slavery to the New World. Secondly, his open relationship with his mistress, Beatriz, was a matter of sexual scandal. Perhaps the final straw was his dishonesty in the matter with Rodrigo Triano. For not only did he steal the 10,000 marevedi that rightfully belonged to this sailor, but he openly used the money to support his mistress in high style. Reluctantly, the Vatican voted down the petition for Columbus' sainthood in 1891.

It is difficult for the entrepreneur to become a saint in any age. Entrepreneur, a French word, is derived from the Latin "inter prendere" which can mean "to take between," which is probably the more generous way to characterize Columbus' efforts, since he attempted "to take his tiny ships between" Scylla and Charbydis and past all the dangers that awaited him as he crossed the open seas of the Atlantic. "Inter prendere" can also mean "to grasp between" or "to seize between," as in the expression "I seized their gold between my hands and ran for home." The entrepreneur seizes at the opportunities that avail themselves and only later has to justify his actions. If his business is successful enough, the profits have a way of providing their own justification.

The venture capitalists can sit back and wait for their ships to come in. If they wish, they can claim ignorance of the methods of those they employ to bring home the wealth that fills up their coffers and finances their churches, their art, and their charities at home. That is, they feel relatively innocent because they did not specifically instruct the entrepreneurs with whom they are associated to engage in deception, enslavement, brutality and terror, nor the wholesale obliteration of cultures and people. Nevertheless, they definitely expect their share of the profits.

On the other hand, the entrepreneurs are wandering throughout the far reaches of a seemingly chaotic world trying to impose capitalist order on people who resist. With the help of pirate adventurers and well-armed overseers and troops from the mother country, the entrepreneurs must impose whatever kind of order, whatever system of forced labor, is necessary to produce the profits. Most of these men are driven by the desperate desire to garner their small proportion of the profits, rather than by sadism. Occasionally, an entrepreneur beats down his competitors, becomes a capitalist himself, and ascends to the level of the rich and cultured. Columbus, who wanted very much to be accepted as a wealthy nobleman at the King's court, was sorely disappointed that he could not amass the riches necessary to attain such status before he died.

Chapter 3

HARD-HEADED BUSINESS - HARD-HEARTED FAITH

1495 - Fierce Spanish dogs were the most valuable employees of Columbus' Enterprise, the most feared enforcers of discipline. They hunted down the Americans who were shirking their work; a few years later they were used to capture the African slaves who managed to escape the plantations.

1495 - Columbus introduced the commerce that would forever change the history of the Americas. He returned to the Spanish Court with a new product line - 500 Indian slaves. They brought a good price, but they rapidly died off in the Spanish winter.

1495 - Because the original Americans chose to resist their rapid deployment in the labor market, they fought back as a group. This required another kind of discipline: Columbus and his brother Bartholemew led a small army of horsemen and soldiers armed with muskets against the Indians. The first war against the rebellious people of the New World lasted about 10 months.

1496 - The first Inquisition in America was performed by a Spanish priest as Bartholemew Columbus watched. Six Indians were burned at the stake for burying images of Jesus and the Virgin Mary in the ground.

HARD-HEADED BUSINESS -
HARD-HEARTED FAITH

The demands of the Europeans were too harsh. Their expectations of profitable production were upset by the extraordinary rate at which the original Americans disappeared:

The Native Population of Hispaniola	
1492-	200,000 to 300,000
1508-	60,000
1512-	20,000
1548-	500

The enslavement of Indians was not a success; the few who went to Europe died too quickly and those who remained in the Caribbean were not surviving their regimen either. The remedy came in 1501 when Columbus and the Spanish on Hispaniola succeeded in getting King Ferdinand's permission to introduce African slave labor to the Caribbean, so that the immense trade in human beings between Africa and America could begin in earnest.

Columbus, like so many Europeans who followed him to the New World, was impatient for his wealth to materialize. This was not just because his dreams of gold, cultivated for so many years in his fertile imagination, had grown wild and unmanageable. He had also made far-fetched promises to the Spanish monarchs in order to launch his voyages. If he didn't return with some proof of the riches residing in the Indies, especially after his second voyage, it was likely that the monarchs would cut off his funds and dismiss him as an incompetent braggart. If harsh measures were required to produce some profits, then Columbus was not going to let scruples stand in his way.

The brutality of Columbus and the Spaniards was not unique; the business enterprises that the white men introduced to America in the following centuries were characterized by haste and impatience. The behavior of the Europeans who expanded capitalism to other parts of the world- Africa, India, Asia, and the East Indies - was more or less identical. If the native people were uncooperative in their labors to extract the wealth, they were disciplined until they complied or died. If the land could not yield up riches with little effort, it would be ransacked quickly and left behind. Such a pattern has been repeated even in our own century, in places so different as the coal fields of Appalachia and the rain forests of Brazil.

FAITH, WAR, AND RATIONALIZATION

Columbus' religious faith helped bolster his certainty that God wanted him to find the westward route to the Indies and it convinced Queen Isabella that Columbus shared her vision of Christianizing the whole world. But faith did more than this, for it also justified the punishment that was meted out to the original Americans by Columbus and his Spanish band.

The natives were not so passive that they let the Spaniards chop off their hands without retaliation. Indian chiefs led raids on Spanish encampments and refused to let their people be abused. To Columbus, this refusal to follow orders was proof of heathen disregard for the wishes of God; in fact, it quickly became specifically against the will of God. The priest who accompanied the Spaniards on the second voyage was employed to denounce the Indians in the name of God and pray for the success of the first war which the Columbus brothers launched against the rebellious infidels in 1495.

It would be a mistake to interpret such religious justification as merely the convenient rationalization for plunder. Columbus and his men believed deeply in both their religion and the superiority of their culture. The intensity of religious passion that had launched the Inquisition and the expulsion of the Jews from Spain in 1492 was also the spirit which led the Spanish priests to force the Indians to accept the European God. It is difficult to overestimate the importance of the unyielding authority of this God: He was called upon to bless the utter submission of the conquered people and to justify their execution as agents of Satan.

Eduardo Galeano has conjectured that the Indians who buried the images of Jesus and Mary were simply experimenting with the efficacy of the new Gods and were using them like they would have used their own Gods; they planted the holy figures in the ground to see if they would bring success in the next harvest. How did they know that a practice that was pious behavior in their own world would be interpreted as a disgusting and vile heresy by the Spaniards?

The religious zeal of the Spanish was not unique to them or to Catholics in general. The European settlement of North America, particularly in New England, was propelled by the Puritan fervor which spilled out of England. The intensity of Puritan belief in England led to the success of Cromwell's revolution and the brutal subjugation and colonization of Catholic Ireland; almost simultaneously in America the Pilgrims' militant faith allowed them to withstand the harsh climate of New England while they pushed the Indians off the land. Governor Winthrop of the Plymouth colony acknowledged that unequal property relations were key to the Pilgrim's endeavors:

> *"God almighty in his most holy and wise providence hath disposed of the Condition of mankind, as in all times some must be rich some poor, some high and eminent in power and dignity; others mean and in subjection."*

And because certain benighted people did not appreciate God's predilection for a hierarchy of property relations, they were ungodly. Winthrop was appalled by the lack of land ownership among the Indians:

> *"That which is common to all is proper to none. This savage people ruleth over many lands without title or property."*

Thus, when the Indians started dying like flies from the smallpox that had been imported from Europe, Winthrop decided God had justified the Englishmen's practice of seizing Indian lands and granting themselves proper deed and title. Of course, the Puritans occasionally chose to help implement God's plan by engaging in their own holy war to eliminate the troublesome residents of America; as John Underhill reported after the English massacred 400 Pequot Indians at Mystic in 1637:

> *"Sometimes the Scripture declareth women and children must perish with their parents... We have sufficient light from the Word of God for our proceedings."*

The notion first unveiled on Columbus' journey, that the European invasion was part of God's plan, became a permanent part of the American dream. Even those who were not so religious in a conventional sense, like Benjamin Franklin, could not help invoking the Authority on High when justifying the theft of land from the Indians. Having helped conclude a treaty with the Indians in 1753 in the middle of frontier Pennsylvania, Franklin chortled over the ease of getting them so drunk that they would sign away their land. He gave credit to alcohol, not smallpox, as God's favorite means of intervention on the white man's behalf:

> *"If it be the design of Providence to extirpate these savages in order to make way for the cultivators of the earth, it seems not impossible that rum may be the appointed means. It has already annihilated all the tribes who formerly inhabited the seacoast."*

When the original Americans were nearly exterminated, and the European-Americans had extended their grasp and control over all the North American continent, the United States was ready to extend its mission as "God's chosen country" across the oceans. Just as Columbus was ready to spread the good news of Queen Isabella's Catholicism to new parts of the world, Protestant North America at the beginning of the 20th century was ready to share the gospel and the ethic of hard work with other parts of the world. President McKinley explained to the Methodist missionary society how he decided that the Americans should conquer the Philippine Islands in 1900:

> *"I went down on my knees and prayed Almighty God... and one night late it came to me this way... there was nothing left for us to do but to take them all... and Christianize them."*

Obviously it had not occurred to McKinley that the Spanish, in their conquest of the Philippines 300 years earlier, had spread the gospel quite thoroughly. Since it was the Catholic version, it apparently did not count as being Christian.

A RAPIDLY CHANGING LABOR FORCE

The Americans who originally populated the Caribbean could not survive the mutilations, the labor speed-up, and the diseases imposed by the European Christians. Oviedo, the Spanish historian who justified the excesses of the conquest, hated the Indians and blamed them for their own demise; he could not imagine why they would choose to die instead of serving the Spanish. He described them as:

> *"so savage that they think everything is in common... people by nature idle and vicious, doing little work. For pastime many killed themselves with venom so as not to work, and others hanged themselves with their own hands."*

Hatuey, an Indian chief on Hispaniola, tried to survive by fleeing the island with some of his people. He canoed to Cuba, hoping to hide there from the savage Europeans. He was captured by the Spanish and was about to be burned at the stake in 1511, when the priest promised him eternal glory and repose in heaven if he would allow himself to be baptized. Hatuey asked:

> *"Are there Christians in that heaven?"*
> *"Yes."*
> *"Then I don't want to go there."*

Oviedo seemed to be angry with the Indians for not surviving the genocidal attack of the Spanish, for the Spanish could not extract profits from these new possessions if their source of slave labor did not survive. The whole population of Mexico,

Central America, the Caribbean, and South America virtually disappeared: there were 65 million Indians in 1492; by 1650 only 3.5 million Indians remained.

Perhaps Columbus had foreseen the problem of the labor shortage when he petitioned King Ferdinand for permission to import slaves from Africa; he had witnessed the success which the Portuguese were already having with sugar plantations in Sao Tomas, the island on the West Coast of Africa. The first African slaves were introduced to the New World in 1502 and by 1516 there were plantation operations of sufficient size to begin the first export of sugar from the New World to Spain. The Africans were not inclined to like their working conditions any more than the Indians had, so they quite promptly rebelled:

1522 - Santo Domingo

The first revolt of African slaves was crushed after they staged a revolt on the plantations of Diego Columbus, son of Christopher, and burned down the sugar mills. The perpetrators and many others were hunted down and the roads of Santo Domingo were lined with hundreds of hanging corpses of men and women - a lesson designed to instill the proper discipline in the mills and the fields.

By 1540 a considerable number of African slaves had been imported to the island of Hispaniola, about 100,000 in all. In future centuries millions and millions of Africans would be brought to America to labor as slaves for the English, the Portuguese, the Dutch, the Prench, and even, to a lesser extent, for the Spanish themselves. But the slave trade started by Columbus slowed down during the 16th century because the Spanish were leaving the Caribbean at too rapid a rate to develop their agricultural assets. But the Spanish were not dying off nor returning to Spain en masse; instead they were racing to Mexico and Peru for the greatest treasure hunt in history.

The Spanish conquests, every bit as brutal as Columbus' conquest of Hispaniola, had begun. They yielded up treasures of gold and silver such as Europe had never seen and elevated Spain to the status as the most powerful nation in Europe for a whole century, during which time these riches were disseminated to the bankers of Germany, Italy, and Holland. This was the moment at which capitalism took off and assumed its non-stop expansion throughout the world. Why did it begin to happen in the 15th century? Michel Beaud, in *The History of Capitalism, 1500-1980*, says:

> *"What was new was the incredible pillage of the Americas."*

Beaud also reminds us that capitalism was not a system that started with small producers and somehow grew into conglomeration of large merchants, national governments, and producers in mines and plantations. Capitalism started as a large worldwide system based on the mass exploitation of labor; it depended upon one continent forcing terms of unequal exchange upon others:

> *"From its first formation, capitalism is national and world wide, private and state based, competitive and monopolistic."*

13

MOUNTAINS OF SILVER AND GOLD

1545 - The Spanish who conquered Peru were led to the solid mountain of silver known as Potosi. In the years to come thousands of Indians were captured each year in distant parts of Peru, Bolivia, and even Chile, and brought to Potosi as slaves. They were lucky to survive for one year.

1573 - Potosi, sitting at about 14,000 feet altitude in the Andes Mountains, had become a city of 120,000 people. It was probably the most expensive city on earth, and certainly the cruelest:

On Sunday morning the Indians emerged from the mines; they drank, they danced, and then they collapsed on the ground.

On Monday morning they were beaten with iron bars and herded into the mountain, where they crept many miles, deeper and deeper into the darkness.

For six days bent over in the dust and the smoke, they mined for silver with their picks and shovels.

On Saturday night the Indians started walking, retracing their steps through the seemingly endless tunnels, so that they might emerge again on Sunday morning.

1600 - A priest who was new in Potosi exclaimed:

"I don't want to see this portrait of hell!"

"So, shut your eyes."

"I can't, with my eyes shut I see even more."

MOUNTAINS OF SILVER AND GOLD

For three centuries after Columbus arrived in America, the "real America" - the America that built up the fortunes of the banks and royal treasure houses of Europe, the America that was an unbelievable fountain of wealth - was Mexico and South America and the West Indies. North America was a backwater until the time of the Revolutionary War. Probably a plantation economy of African slaves, with which Columbus' family and Spanish settlers were experimenting in the Indies in the early 1500s, could have yielded considerable wealth to the Spanish. But they quickly lost interest in such cultivation; settlers became adventurers and rushed to the continents to ransack the great civilizations of the Aztecs in Mexico and the Incas in Peru.

Hernando Cortes had arrived in Hispaniola as an adventurous 19 year old in 1504. By 1519 he was a modestly wealthy landowner and slaveholder who had listened closely as others returned with tales of mysterious wealth on the continent. So, at age 34, Cortes raised a small army and navy to sail to Mexico and march on the capital of the Aztecs. He was welcomed in peace, as if he were a God returned to earth, to Tenochtitlan, that wondrous place that would later become Mexico City. By 1523, Cortes with his armored horsemen and cannons, accompanied by many thousands of Indians from tribes who hated the rule of the Aztecs, had defeated the Aztec armies. When the gold and silver of Mexico was shipped back to Spain, they had never seen such riches. That is, until the wealth of the Incas arrived.

In 1532 Pizarro captured "The Inca," the head of the vast empire of Incas that spanned a good part of the Western side of South America. The ransom paid for the Inca by his followers produced tons of gold and silver which first arrived in Madrid in 1534. These were sufficient to allow the Spanish to pay all their debts and start extending their rule over a good part of the Mediterranean and the continent of Europe. Some have estimated (perhaps exaggerating to make the point) that for every Spanish gentleman who worked in the 16th century, there were thirty who did not. The point being that the stunning enrichment of Spain created a whole new class of noblemen and gentlemen of leisure, and few men who wanted to work, even as bankers. Instead the great bankers of Germany, the Fuggers and the Walsers, and the banking cities of Genoa and Amsterdam handled the fortunes of the Spanish monarchs and circulated this new wealth throughout Europe.

The societies of the original Americans were destroyed everywhere: Indians died in repeated uprisings against their conquerors, from the harshness of the enslavement, and from the spread of diseases like smallpox and typhoid which were new to them. Even where the populations were not exterminated entirely, they dwindled to a small fraction of their former size, leaving demoralized herds of people who were subject to unspeakable tortures and iniquities. Even the conquerors looked back with some sense of shame and lingering admiration for what existed when they arrived on the scene. The land of the Incas, even though it was ruled by harsh monarchs, was a well-ordered and productive one, far superior to the world of degradation that followed. The last survivor of Pizarro's army, Captain Serra de Leguizamo, looked back wistfully on those days and probably with some exaggeration brought on by a sense of guilt:

> *"We discovered the realms in such condition that there was not in all of them one thief, one vicious man, nor idler, nor was there an adulterous or bad woman... the land and the mountains and the mines and the pastures and the hunting grounds and woods and all manner of resources were governed or divided in such a way that everyone knew and had his property, without anyone else occupying or taking it."*

THE MINING ENTERPRISES

The extraordinary thefts of the conquistadors, perhaps the largest in history (did all the armed brigands in history ever carry away as much booty as Cortes and Pizarro?) only supplied a minor portion of the wealth that would flow for the next two centuries from Mexico and Peru to the Spanish court. For although some adventurers would keep seeking imaginary cities of gold for years, the smart investors created a mining industry such as Europe had never seen.

Almost every colonized area of the New World employed slave labor in gold and silver mining operations. In most places, the yield of valuable ore was meager to modest; no matter how much the enslaved Indians and Africans were brutalized, they came up empty-handed panning for gold. Sooner or later the slaves who survived in these areas were transferred to some other kind of work, usually on the plantations.

But on rare occasions the rabid search for precious metal was successful. By the end of the 1500s there was a mining industry in Mexico which would come to rival the production of Potosi. In fact, one city at the center of Mexican mining activity was named San Luis Potosi in honor of the South

American city. The Spaniards rounded up Indians from the seacoasts and the remote regions of the interior; they were often branded with the name of the mine where they were likely to die. In the 1600s and 1700s, the silver mines of Guanajuato and Zacatecas were especially rich:

- The richest mine in Guanajuato, the Valencia, produced 36 times as much as the richest silver mine in Europe, the Himmelsfurst.
- Between 1503 and 1660, 16,000,000 kilograms of silver arrived in Spain. This was three and a half times the silver reserves of all of Europe. (And since it was the official amount counted, it was just a fraction of the total, for great amounts were smuggled to Europe, captured by pirates, and traded directly with China.)

By 1600 Mexico City and Lima, Peru became large, rich metropolises which lacked for none of the culture and luxuries of the cities of Europe. Cathedrals and opera houses were built, carriages paraded through the paved streets, and white ladies made sure they kept their skin out of the sun; all of them, buildings and carriages and women, were ornamented with layers of gold and silver. These cities, and lesser but still substantial regional centers, were the developed part of the American economy. Over two hundred years later, they still dwarfed the little cities in North America at the time of the Revolutionary War. Far from being underdeveloped, the New World to the south of Florida was overdeveloped and overexploited for centuries; only in the late nineteenth century did the industrializing North surpass the wealth churned out by the South.

Potosí, the first great mining center of Peru (in what is now Bolivia) kept yielding extraordinary amounts of silver for two hundred years. In 1670, Count Lemos arrived from Spain as the newly appointed governor of Peru and Bolivia and was so appalled at what he saw that he immediately wrote back to the King:

> *"There is no people in the world so exhausted. It is not silver that is brought to Spain, but the blood and sweat of Indians."*

Count Lemos asked the Council of the Indies in Madrid, the group of noblemen and merchant investors who advised the King on policies in America, to outlaw the forced labor in the mines. They refused, and not just because they knew their sizable incomes depended upon such coercion. Ever since the Spanish had arrived in the New World,

they had claimed that the Indians were inferior creatures who needed stern masters to discipline them and show them the way to salvation. For every protest from someone like Count Lemos, there were ten mine owners to remind the royal commission that such bleeding hearts had little understanding of "reality." The investors at home knew the code words; those who talked of "reality" meant that brutal treatment was the only way to assure the flow of profits.

Furthermore, for almost two centuries the Council of the Indies and the Kings had received advice from priests and learned men. In 1512, Friar Bernardo de Mesa found it easy to justify the enslavement of the Caribbean aborigines:

> *"The Indians were given to the King for their own good, and idleness is their worst possible vice (and all others flow from it.)"*

One priest, Father Gregorio Garcia, detected Semitic blood in the Indians; like the Jews, he said;

> *"they are all lazy, they do not believe in the miracles of Jesus Christ, and they are ungrateful to the Spaniards for all the good they have done them."*

Sepulveda, the famous scholar and chaplain to the King of Spain, advised Charles V that the Bible sanctioned legitimate forms of dominion over one's subjects and just punishment of all the sinners who labored on his behalf. Sepulveda's words were admired by the wealthy men of Mexico City, so their city council voted to send him gold in appreciation of his services.

Charles V, King of Spain and the Emperor of much of Europe in the 16th century, did not necessarily believe such rationalizations of racism and the subjugation of the Indians. There were, now and again, voices of reason grown impassioned by their witness to slaughter and slavery. The greatest of these protestors was the priest, Bartholome de las Casas, a man who had transcribed Columbus' journals and chronicled his voyages to the Indies, and had sailed with him on his third voyage. His writings convinced Charles V to ban the practice of slavery in New Spain, or Mexico, in 1539. Of course, the Spanish gentlemen of Mexico just laughed and put a new brand on their slaves: it said "free." Because it was obvious that the morality of the Spanish in America could not be controlled, especially if it meant limiting the profits which were sent back to Spain, the Council of the Indies convinced the King to reinstate the legality of slavery three years later.

ANOTHER MAGICAL ATTRIBUTE OF CAPITALISM

One must ask how the Spanish in America, as well as the Portuguese, Dutch, French, and English who followed them, were able to subdue the millions of inhabitants who were not willing to become the work animals of Europe. Certainly the message of the priests was not convincing enough to make the Americans lay down their arms, nor was the spread of disease, the greatest killer of all, demoralizing enough to make them don their shackles without a fight. The key for the invaders from Europe was to entice a few of the indigenous people into turning against their brethren.

As the budding capitalists organized their affairs on a transoceanic basis, they also began to conceptualize their business as taking place in a world economy where profit maximization was often preferable to total despotic control over every ally and employee. Hence, from the very beginning, the handful of conquistadors enlisted the help of various Indian tribes in Mexico, those who were either afraid of the power of the Aztecs or already had been defeated by them. The Spanish offered the possibility of avenging past wrongs and taking part in the looting of Aztec treasures. Thus thousands upon thousands of Indian troops were organized by Cortes for the final conquest of Mexico. Later, in the 18th and 19th centuries, much the same strategy was employed by the British in other parts of the world that fed their vast empire-most notably in India where they employed their own armies of native troops.

But beyond the thirst for revenge, primitive capitalism promised benefits to those who would become intermediaries in the process of securing labor. The magic trick of capitalism was to pay semi-autonomous people for their services, turning them into sub-contractors for labor who could deliver the goods (fresh slaves) by whatever means they felt were necessary. The Paulistas were one example of a marginal group which wanted to show its prowess and earn a large measure of independence in service to the plantation owners of Brazil.

The Paulistas, or "bandeiristas" as they were also called, lived in the region of Sao Paolo and were the mixed-race offspring of Portuguese plantation owners, Indians, African slaves, and various castoffs from Europe. The Paulistas specialized in delivering fresh Indian slaves to the plantations on the Atlantic Coast of Brazil and staged hunting expeditions, called "bandeiras," over vast areas of South America, waging merciless raids on Indian villages and returning with their human booty. It is estimated that they captured over two million slaves for the plantations; sometimes they spent two years on just one "bandeira" expedition into the interior of the continent. The Paulistas were such fierce and reckless warriors that the Portuguese rulers begged for their assistance in the jungle of Northern Brazil, where African slaves had escaped and incorporated their own little nation called Palmares. After the Portuguese and Dutch armies had been defeated by these Africans in several wars over a period of nearly a hundred years, the Paulistas were hired to take over the task of eliminating this refuge of the black slaves. They succeeded within a year.

The magic of capital for the Europeans was that it allowed them to call on resources and arrange alliances on a scale unknown in the Americas and in most of the rest of the world. The tribal cultures might win one battle and think that, as in a skirmish with an old tribal rival, the war would not be rejoined for some time. But for the early European capitalists war was something else, another tool of coercion which they could purchase and keep applying until the necessary result was achieved. It was not so difficult to corrupt marginal groups like the Paulistas with a small share in the proceeds derived from this coercion. The superior arms of the Europeans and the religious justifications which they spread were certainly effective means of enforcing their desires; but probably just as valuable for the spread of European control were the organized greed and contagious self-interest of their economic system.

The power of capitalism, said Marx, was demonstrated by its ability to overwhelm the kinds of human relations that previously held sway in various countries and continents, and to enshrine the essence of bourgeois European values throughout the world. The new values, said Marx:

"left no other nexus between man and man than naked self-interest, than callous 'cash payment.'"

17

SLAVERY: THE WEALTH OF EUROPE

The plantations... were capitalist creations par excellence: money, credit, trade and exchange tied them to the east side of the Atlantic. Everything was remote - controlled from Seville, Cadiz, Bordeaux, Nantes, Rouen, Amsterdam, Bristol, and Liverpool.

- Fernand Braudel, *Civilization and Capitalism*

At the heart of plantation production was slavery, which required the development of racist classifications for maintaining long- term distinctions between the owners and the owned:

AT THE SLAVE MARKET: GRADATIONS OF COLOR

Racial Category	% of "Blackness"	Parentage
Black or Negro	100%	African parents
Mulatto	50%	black and white
Sambo	75%	black and mulatto
Quadroon	25%	mulatto and white
Mustee (or Octaroon)	12.5%	quadroon and white
Musteefino	6.25%	mustee and white

(distinctions used in the slave markets of Kingston, Jamaica in the 18th century)

SLAVERY: THE WEALTH OF EUROPE

In the process of enriching Europe, the plantation system of agriculture became even more important than the mining and plunder of gold and silver. Racism, the systematic dehumanizing of African Americans and native Americans, has been central to the whole development of "Western" (meaning European) culture and economy in the New World. This color line was not originally created out of irrational prejudice, but rather from coldly rational calculation. Color, even in the slightest degree, was for sale; that is, anyone "of color" could be classified as a slave and traded as a valuable beast of burden. Women of child-bearing age were frequently the most expensive slaves because they could simultaneously work in the fields and reproduce more slaves.

Slavery was not the invention of 15th and 16th century European capitalists any more than the murderous pillage of the Spaniards in America was something new and horrible in a previously benign world. Many human cultures had practiced degrees of slavery, particularly after capturing enemy soldiers in wars and skirmishes. What was new with the early stages of capitalist development was the scale at which slavery for profit was extended throughout the world and made part of the very soul of world trade. The sustained ruthlessness of exploitation and brutalization which forced the servitude of millions of families for many generations only made sense when attached to the logic of property ownership and systematic profit-taking which spanned centuries and kept spreading throughout the world. Ultimately the development of capitalism, which became dependent in its advanced industrial form on wage labor, made most slavery obsolete.

Nonetheless, slavery in America was a feature of the primitive capitalism which would later finance industrial capitalism, or as Karl Marx put it:

> *"The veiled slavery of the wage-workers in Europe needed, for its pedestal, slavery pure and simple in the New World."*

DYING FOR SUGAR

After an initial burst of African slave importation in the 16th century, the development of slavery in the Caribbean was delayed by the Spanish preoccupation with the Conquests. Thus, during that century, slaves were primarily imported to Brazil, where the Portuguese set up extensive sugar cane plantations up and down the long Atlantic Coast of the country. At first Indians were rounded up and forced into slavery on the plantations, but, just as in the Caribbean, their mortality rate was so great that their numbers were depleted very quickly. Since the Portuguese were already using slave labor on islands off the coast of Africa, they began transporting these African slaves across the Atlantic.

By 1600 these plantations in Brazil fed cane into 120 sugar mills. In the 16th, 17th, 18th and 19th centuries, Africans were shipped across the ocean to cut Brazilian cane, work on other kinds of plantations, and, after gold was discovered just before 1700, to work in the mines. Just how many slaves were transported to the New World is a matter of debate:

- The historian Giao Prado has estimated that 6,000,000 Africans were transported to Brazil before 1800. (And slavery was not outlawed there until 1880.)

- The figure given by the historian Ferdnand Braudel: 17,000,000 slaves imported to the entire New World.

- A conservative estimate from Philip Curtin: 10 million slaves arrived alive in the Americas. (On the other hand, Basil Davidson and other historians of Africa have estimated that at least 50 million Africans died as a result of slave hunting raids and while in transit to America.)

From 1550 to 1650 the English and the French began to gradually populate their possessions in the New World, yet their first sources of exploited labor were not African slaves, but rather indentured servants or convicts who were brought from Europe. Life was cruel for these people, who often succumbed to the combination of overwork, poor nutrition, and disease. Often the indentured servants were poor children who had been kidnapped off the streets of English and French port cities; sometimes religious wars produced a short-term supply of prison laborers: in 1651 7,000 to 8,000 Scots were taken prisoner by Cromwell's Puritan armies at the Battle of Worcester and sent to the plantations to work. The first plantations organized in Virginia after the founding of Jamestown in 1607 were, in fact, forced labor camps dependent on indentured servants. Those who profited by such forced labor found it easy to justify the practice; Josiah Child, in his *New Discourse on Trade* in 1668, wrote:

> *"Virginia and Barbados were first peopled by a sort of loose vagrant people, vicious and destitute of the means to live at home These, had there been no English foreign plantation in the world, must have come to be hanged or starved."*

There were three problems with indentured servants, however. There was a limited supply of those who could be forced or fooled into coming to America; the terms of their indenture were limited to a relatively short time - often four, five, or eight years - after which they had to be set free; finally, since they were white Europeans, they could often escape and pass for freemen entitled to farm their own land. The colonists decided to learn from the example of the Portuguese and the Dutch and take advantage of an unlimited supply of labor of a distinctly different color: the Africans.

By the early 1600s the primary financiers of Brazilian sugar plantations in the Northeast states of Brazil were Dutchmen. Tiny Holland was then enjoying its brief tenure as the center of the new international economic system; as the undisputed master of mercantile capitalism, the city of Amsterdam (like London and New York in later times) controlled most international trading, shipping, and banking. The slave trade with Africa was now dominated by the ships from Holland, too. The sugar plantations made their way north with Dutch businessman who helped the English set up the first slave plantations in the Caribbean.

The transformation of Barbados is instructive of the incredible power of capitalist investment to transform the nature of agricultural and social life. In 1645 Barbados was a small island already well-populated by European immigrant farmers, predominately English, who were small-scale proprietors of self-sufficient farms which exported modest amounts of various products to England. Enjoying this comfortable life were 18,300 whites, most of whom were proprietors, with a minority being employees or indentured servants; with them were a modest number of African slaves, 5,680. Within twenty years small-scale agriculture was virtually wiped out by the capitalist wave of plantation agriculture:

The Capitalist Transformation of Barbados

1645	1667
18,300 whites	6,500 whites
5,680 slaves	82,023 slaves
11,200 proprietors	745 plantation owners
10 acre farms	300 acre plantations

The experience of Barbados shows that even a well-colonized little island could be transformed overnight by the logic of capitalist investment. Barbados became so overdeveloped that its slave population of 82,023 (on a territory of 166 square miles) was nearly as great as the entire European colonial population of the United States, which was 111,900 in 1670. In 1697 tiny Barbados was the most important English colony by far; its trade with England was almost equal to that of the colonies of Virginia and Maryland combined.

By the 18th century, however, the soil of Barbados had been severely wasted by the monoculture of sugar, and so it was left behind by the development of the much larger island of Jamaica, which had fresh soils capable of greater productivity per acre. Jamaica was the most important English colony in the whole world, surpassing even the vast subcontinent of India in the late 18th century.

On the eve of the Revolutionary War in the United States the value of imports from the West Indies far exceeded that from the North American mainland:

Value of Exports to England in 1775

from West Indies	from North America
£101,264,818	£55,552,675

This wealth was purchased at an immense cost of human life. One 18th century calculation of slave mortality shows:

- 16% of African slaves died on board the slave ships
- 33% of those remaining died within three years
- for every 56 slaves alive on plantations three years after shipping out from Africa, 44 had died.

The sugar plantation based on slave labor was the ultimate in capitalist production in the 18th century. Adam Smith recognized that it produced far more return on capital than other types of agricultural investment:

> *"The profits of the sugar plantation are generally much greater than any other cultivation that is known either in Europe or America."*

Charles Davenant, a highly respected 17th century British economist, estimated that each individual working in the West Indies was worth 7 times as much as one in England. And the British prime minister Postlethwayt declared that the British Empire was:

> *"A magnificent superstructure of American commerce and naval power [built] on an African foundation."*

The English were not alone in their assiduous cultivation of the New World; the French colony of Saint Domingue (where Haiti is today) created more wealth in the 18th century than all the

English Indies combined. The French monarchs had realized the potential of slavery and Louis the XIV had decreed in 1670:

"There is nothing which contributes more to the development of the colonies and the cultivation of their soil than the laborious toil of the Negroes."

The trade in millions of kidnapped people was nearly as enriching as the sugar trade - the Dutch, who dominated the world's oceans for roughly a century, from 1550 to 1650, took over leadership in the slave trade from the Portuguese. By the mid-17th century, many European countries - Portugal, Holland, England, France, Denmark, Sweden, and Germany - had established their own export companies complete with African trading forts erected for the purpose of dealing in human flesh.

The Spanish found a way to make considerable profit on the slave trade by making Asientos, or contracts, with other Europeans who wanted to sell their slaves in the Spanish possessions. The Spanish king received a certain percentage of the price brought by each slave in the New World markets.

In 1685 the Council of the Indies in Madrid went to great lengths to convince the Spanish monarchs of the religious propriety of continuing this kind of slave trade; one solution was to send Spanish priests along with the Protestant Dutch sea captains to the shores of Africa. There the priests could convert the slaves to Catholicism before they were transported to the New World.

The systematic enslavement of Africans, like the extermination of the original Americans, was not sanctioned by everyone. A French Dominican missionary named du Tertre tried to expose the cruelties of slavery to the people of France. He realized that there was something deeper than color prejudice underlying their degradation, something nearly impossible to eliminate because of the economic advantages which the planters enjoyed in the New World. He said that it would be easier to ask the rich in France to renounce all their worldly goods than to ask the sugar planters to abolish "the shameful commerce, sale and purchase of their fellow men."

The Protestant counterpart to this opposition to slavery was best expressed by the English Quakers, who preached freedom for the slaves in Barbados. Some Quakers even did the unthinkable; they freed their slaves and divided the land among them. Other Englishmen on Barbados were so fearful of the Quakers' example that in 1676 the government banned attendance by Negroes at all Quaker meetings.

Chapter 6

WHO OPPOSED GENOCIDE IN THE NEW WORLD?

The European conquest of America was the greatest human disaster that the world has ever known.

The indigenous population of the New World almost disappeared:
        1492: 72,000,000   1900: 3,500,000

At the same time, Europe prospered and its population multiplied:
        1492: 65,000,000   1900: 400,000,000

In the 1500s the priest Bartolome de las Casas defended the Indians and denounced the Spanish colonists:

"Those who for greed turn Jesus Christ into the cruelest of Gods."

In the early 1800s Father Miguel Hidalgo, who lived and worked among the Indians, led a huge army of the poor and dispossessed against the Spanish and the rich white creoles of Mexico. Their battle cry was:

"Long live America! Long live Independence! Death to Bad Government!"

WHO OPPOSED GENOCIDE IN THE NEW WORLD?

We have already noted how important it has been for each European nationality at each stage of the European conquest to justify its pillage and murder as a religious mission; that is, they were working for the greater glory of God. Christianity quickly came to dominate the life of the American continents; the social structure and activities of everyday life had their justifications in religious logic. Thus, the depredations in the New World had to be forced to fit into this religious logic as best they could, usually on the pretense of saving the souls of the damned.

Those Europeans who resisted the rationalization of murder in the name of God were relatively few and seldom successful in their struggles, but they were usually religious people themselves and faith was their primary weapon. One reason that a few unarmed people caused so much consternation for the owners of plantations and mines, for both those who whipped the slaves in the New World and those who counted the profits from slave labor in the Old, was that the power of Christian morality lay on their side. Although they seldom won the struggle for human dignity, the tradition of these religious protestors has been passed down in the present day to the practitioners of liberation theology, who preach that God favors the poor and oppressed of the earth. In fact, this new breed of Christians really believes in Jesus' vision, that "the meek shall inherit the earth."

LAS CASAS: THE "PROTECTOR OF THE INDIANS"

When Bartolome de las Casas arrived in America in 1502, he was one of many settlers accompanying Columbus on his third voyage, just another 28 year old Spaniard in search of his fortune. In those early years, he quickly acquired land and mines which were worked by his own Indian slaves; he was also studying to be a priest, a duty which did not prevent him from continuing to enjoy the ease of plantation life. In 1511, he heard the Dominican friar, Antonio de Montesinos, give a scorching condemnation of the Spaniards' treatment of their Indian slaves:

"Aren't you killing them, to get gold every day? Aren't you obliged to love them as yourselves?"

These words were a revelation that changed the life of Las Casas. For the next 50 years he was to fight valiantly, often futilely, to save the Indians.

He was also the first historian of the New World, the man who collected, corrected, and edited the diaries of Columbus. A great admirer of the navigator, he tended to forgive him for introducing slavery because he felt Columbus had been chosen by God to find the New World so that the Indians could be converted to the Christian faith.

Las Casas believed that Christianization meant nothing unless the Indians were treated as fully human beings. He wrote in a letter to the Council of the Indies in Madrid that:

"the cries of so much blood reach all the way to heaven: those burned alive, roasted on grills, thrown to wild dogs."

Such atrocities committed in the name of God were so horrible, Las Casas added, that it might be better for these unlucky Indians—

"to go to hell with their heresies, their procrastination, and their isolation"

—rather than be saved by such Christians as the Spanish.

The pleas of Las Casas helped convince Pope Paul III to issue a papal bull, the *Sublimis Deus* of 1537, which revealed that the Indians were true human beings, possessed of both souls and the ability to reason with their brains. By 1542 Las Casas' treatise, *A Brief Account of the Destruction of the Indies*, had influenced the King of Spain, who then sent mandates to America requiring the humane treatment of the Indians. Such was the uproar in America, where the owners of plantations and mines detested Las Casas as a meddling idealist, that the King retracted the order three years later.

Later Las Casas' *Destruction of the Indies* was translated into various languages and used to discredit the Spanish. Richard Hakluyt, the Anglican priest in England who did so much to encourage the English crown to create an American Empire of its own, used passages of from Las Casas in his "Discourse on Western Planting" (1584) in order that he might invoke "a proper horror of Spain" in Queen Elizabeth. This seemed to be for propaganda purposes only, since Elizabeth had already decided in 1564 that the English mariners should be allowed to engage in the very lucrative trade in slaves between Africa and America.

From that time the Spanish crown made certain that most of Las Casas' works, including his lengthy *History of the Indies*, were hidden away in a Spanish monastery so that the enemies of Spain could not find more ammunition to attack the Spanish character. His historical work remained unknown for three hundred years.

THE JESUITS: PROVIDING REFUGE FOR THE INDIANS

If Las Casas was the single most effective opponent of slavery and the genocide practiced against the Indians, then a small number of Jesuit priests who settled in South America were the most resolute group in their attempts to counteract the slaughter wreaked upon the disappearing Americans.

The Society of Jesus settled its members in many locales throughout the New World. In some places they were large landowners who exploited Indian labor or imported African slaves, but sometimes they tried to convince the European invaders to ameliorate the inhuman conditions in which the Indians were forced to live. When their efforts were spurned, certain priests began to set up their own separate colonies for the indigenous people in remote parts of South America. This particular Jesuit model was a utopian version of the primitive communism of the early Christian communities mentioned in the Bible; it also drew upon two of the most influential books of the 16th century, *Utopia* by Thomas More and *The City of the Sun* by Tomaso Campanella, which suggested that humankind could remake the world and produce a new society.

Eduardo Galeano, in *Memories of Fire*, describes their efforts in Paraguay with the Guarani Indians:

> *"Under the priests' tutorship the Guaranis share a regimented life, without private property or money or death penalty, without luxury or scarcity, and march to work singing to the music of flutes."*

> *"The Jesuits had taught them to make clocks, plows, bells, clarinets, and books printed in their Guarani language."*

The localities which would permit this utopian program were very limited, however. Because the Jesuits in Brazil opposed both slavery and the indentured labor of Indians bound to their Spanish masters, Indians fled to them for protection. Obviously the labor supply for mining and agriculture was effected, so the Jesuits were quickly attacked by the colonial governors. Some groups, like the Paulistas in Brazil, saw the Jesuits' activities as directly opposed to their economic survival. How were they to engage in successful slave raids if the Jesuits first opposed their efforts, then offered refuge to those who escaped the system of bondage?

The Paulistas expelled the Jesuits from their own province of Sao Paulo. This led the Society of Jesus to concentrate its efforts in Paraguay, which in the early 1600s was a very large and vague area stretching South of Brazil (Argentina had not yet been founded) and west of Southern Brazil as far as present day Bolivia.

The Jesuits started communities in Guaira (two Italian priests who were influenced by Campanella were the founders) on the Parana River and were successful in using peaceful means to lure the Guarani Indians to live with them in areas called "reducciones." Rather quickly large towns with varied agriculture and simple handiworks flourished and operated on a system of trust, complete equality and an absence of money. In the early years there was only one problem: the mass of people were unarmed and prey to attacks by the slave raiders of Sao Paulo, who realized they could capture Indians much more easily, 5,000 or 10,000 at a time, by concentrating on the Jesuit communities.

In self-defense, the Jesuits resorted to manufacturing guns, arming the Indians in the new communities, and training them into sophisticated forces of cavalry and musketeers. The Indians succeeded in repeatedly repulsing the raids of the Paulistas; because of their renown as soldiers, they were then called upon to help defend the weak armies of the Spanish colonists in Argentina. The success of the utopian communities proved to be their undoing: their widespread cultivated lands, their handsome towns, and productive industries became the envy of both the Portuguese in Brazil and the Spanish immigrants to the South.

As one of the last havens of the decimated Indian population which sought to avoid slavery, the Jesuit Reducciones were the antithesis of the general pattern of economic development in South America. As if to emphasize this fact, the King of Spain decided to present his father-in-law, the King of Portugal, with a gift of seven of the finest Guarani villages. In 1754 the Jesuits of Paraguay refused to relinquish these Reducciones and as a result the Indians had to fight off several armies sent by both crowns; ultimately their villages were destroyed by the invaders. In 1767 the governments of Spain and Portugal were so incensed at the interference of the Jesuits that they expelled the whole order from their home countries; then the Spanish authorities arrested over two thousand priests in the New World and shipped them back to Italy. The Spanish and Portuguese monarchs began to prevail upon the Vatican to the extent that the Pope soon dismantled the Jesuit order throughout the whole world.

Modern Jesuits, having rebuilt their order in the 19th century, look back on their New World experiment with some embarrassment because, for all the communitarian brotherhood promoted in their "reducciones," the Indians were always under the paternalistic control of a handful of Jesuit priests. Never quite allowed to escape their treatment as "innocent children," the Indians were not equipped to withstand the onslaught of the European colonists when the Jesuits were forced to leave them behind. Still, whatever the limitations of their time, the Jesuits in Paraguay were effective in creating a much more humane model of life in the New World, one of the few places where the original Americans could survive with dignity. Montesquieu, who was no lover of the Catholic church, commented:

"The Society of Jesus may pride itself on the fact that it was the first to prove to the world that religion and humanity are compatible."

PRIESTS AS REVOLUTIONARIES

In the 19th century, the moral outrage of Las Casas and the utopian logic of the Jesuits were joined by a third thread of religious defiance of the worldly order: the right of the oppressed to overthrow their oppressors. In 1810, in Mexico, two rural priests, Hidalgo and Morelos, led revolutionary movements of Indians and mestizos against the rule of the Spanish. Marching at the head of huge armies of the poor and disenfranchised, Hidalgo and Morelos gathered forces that swept over much of Mexico. They frightened the Spanish crown and many wealthy creoles, the white citizens of Mexico who favored independence under their own bourgeois state. The radical priests and their followers proposed:

- Independence from Spain
- An income tax in place of Indian tributes
- An end to the color line between Indians, mestizos, and whites
- The outlawing of slavery and torture
- The recovery of Indian lands
- Some confiscation of the goods of the Europeans

Although both Hidalgo and Morelos were captured and tortured by Inquisitors, then executed as infidels and traitors to both God and the King of Spain, they set yet another precedent for those religious people who opposed the inequities of the social order in the Americas. The ideas of equality and human dignity had reached Father Hidalgo through the world of books, especially the works of the French Enlightenment; when dean of a seminary he was removed by church authorities for spreading liberal ideas among the students. He was demoted to service in an Indian village where he oversaw the making of pottery and began to dream of actively changing history. Morelos, once a student at Hidalgo's seminary, had previously worked as a driver of oxen and small-time trader. As a practically-minded man of the people, he became a talented military organizer whose army struck great fear in the hearts of the conservative church and its allies. When the historical example of these priests filtered through to the 20th century, it was instrumental in promoting the Mexican Revolution and nourishing a widespread feeling of anticlericalism, a kind of revenge against the reactionary Church structure which had punished Hidalgo and Morelos.

The example of Hidalgo and Morelos has been followed by 20th century priests and ministers throughout the Americas - from Brazil to Chile, from Columbia to Mexico, from Nicaragua to El Salvador - who have chosen various means of allying themselves with "the people." The "people," of course, are the vast majority of Americans, the brown-skinned people on whose backs the development of the Hemisphere has rested for centuries. Today the tradition of religious activism in America is expressed in cooperatives in the countryside and labor unions in the cities, through support for Christian "base communities" and peaceful social revolution. The nature of this struggle is best expressed in the words of Morelos:

"America is free even if we do not seem to be..."

Part II

THE CAPITALIST CONQUEST OF CENTRAL AMERICA

The wretchedly poor Americans who pick the coffee beans and cut the sugar cane for the wealthy nations of the world do not do so happily or even passively. For five hundred years, since the Indians of Hispaniola first resisted the forced labor imposed by Columbus, the oppressed have dreamed of freedom and they have repeatedly rebelled.

If we look briefly at some of the recent history of Central America and the conditions under which people live, it becomes clear that capitalist development in America does not mean more material progress for most people. In the second half of the 20th century, life has been getting more wretched for most citizens, and infinitely more brutal for everyone. In Central America, the small size of the countries and their proximity to the United States makes them more easy to manipulate than other nations in the Hemisphere. The harsh rule of local oligarchies is tied to a larger system of capitalist control. The methods of external control, as exemplified by CIA-inspired military coups, and internal control, like para-military "death squads," were first developed in Central America and then used elsewhere in Latin America.

Today Central America is being more thoroughly integrated into the international economy and has various kinds of business connections with the United States and the capitalist system in general. Although the agricultural export economy based on plantations has continued to grow and is still predominant, there is now considerable activity by transnational industrial corporations, which import manufactured goods and set up manufacturing operations for new exports. Since more and more peasants are without land because of agro-business expansion, they flee to the capital cities, which are overflowing with unemployed refugees who are willing to work for almost nothing. In El Salvador these workers are paid ultra-low wages to sew Maidenform bras and Levi Strauss jeans. In Guatemala they might work for U.S. pharmaceutical manufacturers or assemble parts for Korean companies. These firms, which pay their own exploited employees in Korea less than $2.00 an hour, can engage in super- exploitation in Guatemala where they pay people less than $2.00 per day.

Throughout Latin America the model of internal domination that allowed the elite to maintain control over their restive populations was based on three pillars: the oligarchy, which consolidated ownership and power in the hands of a few families; the military, whose complicity in enforcing authority by all possible means was required to maintain social order; and the Catholic Church, whose conservative ideological hegemony taught the people to obey the oligarchical and military powers no matter what. Since the 1960s, however, the third pillar has weakened considerably and even crumbled in some countries.

Under the influence of "liberation theology," many religious people began to work openly on behalf of poverty-stricken peasants and workers in Central America who were already influenced by nationalistic revolutionary impulses, practical experience in unions and cooperatives, and a Marxist analysis of their economic and social situation. The oligarchies had to resort more and more to overt repression in their attempts to control their uncooperative citizens. Their inability to impose even greater subservience upon their populations led to war in El Salvador, Nicaragua, Guatemala, and Honduras. Vast military assistance from the United States, both direct and indirect, was necessary to prop up the old power structure and hasten the further integration of the Central American economies into the larger capitalist marketplace.

In the following chapters, as we look at the rebellion of the Central Americans and the escalating repressive measures of those who want to control them, we will also examine the battle for ideological hegemony that accompanies the political and economic struggle. Catholic thought, because of the influence of liberation theology, is now an unreliable ally or a subversive agent from the point of view of capitalist hegemony. Therefore there is room for new religious and ideological forces, one of which is fundamentalist Americanism, the pro-capitalist belief structure of the Religious Right in the United States which has been energetically exported to the growing Protestant churches of Central and Latin America.

Chapter 7

WHAT IF THEY STOPPED BRINGING YOUR CUP OF COFFEE IN THE MORNING?

1932 - In El Salvador, the peasants tried to overthrow the few rich coffee growers who controlled the economy and the government. This was the first attempt at making a socialist revolution in the Western Hemisphere.

1980 - Archbishop Romero of El Salvador, who had been chosen for his post because he was considered a moderate who would not offend the ruling class, was assassinated because he decided to side with the poor. He said:

"The cause of our problems is the oligarchy, that tiny group of families which has no concern for the hunger of the people, but in fact needs it in order to have cheap and abundant labor to export its crops."

1989 - Six Jesuits priests who called for peace talks between the revolutionaries and the military were exterminated by an Army death squad which had received U.S. training in "unconventional warfare."

WHAT IF THEY STOPPED BRINGING YOUR CUP OF COFFEE IN THE MORNING?

In 1932 El Salvador's economy was based on coffee plantations controlled by the "Fourteen Families" who owned almost all of the productive land. Coffee made up 95% of the country's exports. When the Great Depression ruined the world coffee market, thousands of peasants were dismissed from work and faced starvation. The peasants rebelled under the leadership of a communist organizer named Farabundo Marti. They began taking control of rural villages and threatened to seize the idle land of the idle rich.

The Salvadoran Army and the national police were able to round up the ringleaders and stop this fledgling revolution in its infancy. Then, to make sure the campesinos had learned their lesson, the Army slaughtered 30,000 suspected sympathizers while a U.S. Navy ship watched approvingly from the coast.

The Salvadoran Army, accompanied by groups of "upper-class gentlemen volunteers," hunted down the victims in a remorseless fashion described in Thomas Anderson's book on the "Matanza:"

> *"Men were taken in big batches, tied together by their thumbs, and lined up along the roadsides or up against the walls of the military forts and churches. They were machine-gunned and their bodies hauled off to makeshift mass graves... The extermination was so great that they could not be buried fast enough and a great stench of rotting flesh permeated the air of western El Salvador."*

Military dictatorships kept order for the next 50 years on behalf of the oligarchy. By the 1980s coffee was still El Salvador's major product, providing 57% of its export earnings. Most of the nation's 5,000,000 people were rural agriculture workers with little or no land; 70% of them lived in absolute poverty - that is, various international development organizations reported that these Salvadorans could not afford to buy or grow food that would meet even the barest nutritional requirements for a daily diet. Things were worse than in 1932: other agro-export industries, like cotton and beef cattle, had taken over even more of the meager land that had once been used to feed the working population. Now more than 40% of the rural peasants had no land at all.

As the 1980s began, the poor people of El Salvador tried again to make a revolution; their determination was so great that even massive aid from the United States could not defeat them. For more than a decade, they have held the Salvadoran oligarchy and the United States Government at bay. The revolutionaries called themselves the Faramundo Marti Liberation Movement, or FMLN, after the leader of the 1932 rebellion. The Salvadoran people were not being led astray by subversive agents of Cuba and Nicaragua, as U.S. propagandists have claimed, for they had their own established revolutionary tradition. But no doubt they were encouraged by the success of the revolutions that had already occurred elsewhere.

This time the poor had new allies - priests and other religious people who supported the right of oppressed citizens to fight back against the evils inflicted upon them. Within the Catholic Church, a significant portion of the clergy had radically deviated from its traditional role of supporting the rich and asking the poor to suffer in silence and await their rewards in heaven. Rather than justifying the exploitation and oppression of the poor peasants and workers as "the will of God," as the traditional Church had done for centuries, the "liberation" church supported the struggle of the oppressed to escape poverty and to control their own destinies.

A SPECIAL TIME IN HISTORY

The conflict in El Salvador marked the convergence of three strong trends that had been developing in the second half of the 20th century in Central and South America. The first of these trends is opposed by the other two:

1. There was the continuing expansion of the international capitalist economic system, which in Central America was building up a large scale apparatus of export agriculture controlled by a combination of local capitalist oligarchs, wealthy foreign investors, and giant transnational corporations.

2. A wide diffusion of Marxist ideas of economic analysis and political organizing informed the poverty-stricken masses that they were the victims of the economic logic of capitalist organization on a world scale.

3. The growth of liberation theology encouraged religious people to ally themselves, usually peacefully, with political movements of liberation.

The oppressed laborers of the New World - be they conquered Indians, African slaves, white servants held in temporary bondage, or industrial workers denied the right to unionize - have always been at least semi-conscious of their exploitation; they knew that a few owners somewhere, whether they were called "capitalists" or not, were profiting from their work. For these peasants and workers to gain more political understanding at the same time that they were given a new kind of spiritual support by the Church is a terribly threatening development for those who gain the most from the present economic arrangements. Thus, at the end of this century, the oligarchy of El Salvador, allied with the capitalist classes, or "bourgeoisie," around the world, is fiercely defending the property rights and privileges which it has enjoyed since the time of the Spanish conquest. The slaughter of peasants and the assassination of priests, nuns, and even the Archbishop, indicate the precariousness of the upper class' position. The barbarity engendered by dreams of wealth in Hispaniola 500 years ago is still alive in the hearts of wealthy Salvadorans.

The "Fourteen Families" are predominantly descendants of the Spanish conquerors and other European settlers who monopolized the export agriculture of El Salvador. For one hundred and fifty years coffee has been the most important export of the plantations; before that cacao beans were exported to chocolate producers and indigo was sent to make dye for the textile industries of Mexico and Europe. As the international export economy has expanded in recent years, as the import of chemicals, fertilizers, and luxury goods for the rich has increased, and because certain military generals have demanded their portion of the booty, the "Fourteen families" have expanded. Still, the Salvadoran oligarchy represents a tiny portion of the population: 114 family groups can be identified which include 1,309 individuals, each having declared capital of $400,000 or more. There is little distinction between families who own the agricultural wealth and those who enter into partnership with U.S. transnational corporations to set up subsidiary industrial ventures in El Salvador. 40% of the country's largest 1,429 business firms are owned by the 36 largest landowning families.

Although a good part of the oligarchy has its roots in the 500 year old Spanish landholding tradition, the real focus of their allegiance today is the United States. The elite are now cosmopolitan bourgeoisie of the world capitalist class; they speak English and fly their own planes to visit their children at American universities. As a former deputy director of the Salvadoran Agrarian Transformation Institute said,

"The oligarch you see in London, in Miami, he plays golf with your cousin in Palm Beach, he has a daughter at Vassar, he has a Playboy subscription, he's one of the boys."

THE PRESENT POLITICAL SITUATION

The United States spent about $1 billion per year in the 1980s to support the military and the oligarchy in El Salvador, but could not defeat the revolutionaries who occupied one third of the country despite heavy bombing by U.S. supplied planes and helicopter gunships. The heavy presence of the United States has forced the oligarchy to present a facade of democratic elections rather than ruling directly through military dictatorships as it did in the past. The President in 1990, Alfredo Cristiani, past head of both the coffee growers' and the cotton growers' associations, came to prominence in the far right ARENA party.

The real leader of the ARENA party, who arranged for Cristiani to be president, is ex-Army major Roberto D'Aubuisson. For years D'Aubuisson has been linked to the fascist secret societies and the death squads that have meted out the ultimate in Salvadoran justice. The fascist societies, with their "white" racist consciousness, have existed throughout Latin America since the days of Adolph Hitler and their names evoke Nazi memories: ORDEN, The White Warriors League, and Mano Blanca (White Hand.) D'Aubuisson was a leader of the White Warriors when they threatened to exterminate the Jesuits in 1977:

The Jesuits' crime: *"Communist support of the poor."*

D'Aubuisson is also the man reputed to have ordered the assassination of Archbishop Romero in 1980. Robert White, who was U.S. ambassador at the time, has called D'Aubuisson a "pathological killer." D'Aubuisson gave that impression in 1982 when he said to a group of European journalists:

"You Germans are very intelligent; you realized that the Jews were responsible for the spread of Communism and you began to kill them."

The Faribundo Marti Front For National Liberation was organized by a coalition of left opposition groups in November of 1980, when there seemed to be no choice but to go underground and begin an armed insurrection against the oligarchy and the military. Many of those who joined the guerrilla movement were refugees from various groups who had tried for years to oppose the corrupt military regimes through peaceful means: labor organizations, teachers' associations, Christian base communities, peasants' leagues, workers' cooperatives, and democratic left political parties. All of these groups were, and still are today, the targets of murder and torture at the hands of the death squads.

Catholic Church representatives did not wake up one day and decide to ally themselves with Marxist guerrillas. Instead, they had been working for twenty years with a number of grassroots political movements: workers' associations in the poor neighborhoods of the cities and peasant groups in the countryside. As they struggled to help the poor improve their lives, they saw their "compañeros" becoming more and more frequent victims of oligarchic vengeance; then they, too, were targeted as the enemy.

A particular threat to the established authority was posed by the "base communities," which were Christian discussion groups led by priests, nuns, or Catholic lay workers. The base communities were a new democratic version of the Church which encouraged poor people to speak up about their lives, to find inspiration for social change in the Bible, and to organize to oppose the forces that oppressed them. Because the base communities were so effective at combining intellectual and spiritual understanding with political understanding of the brutality of the Salvadoran class system, their leaders were singled out; a number of priests and nuns, including four American women, as well as a much greater number of Salvadoran lay workers, were murdered.

Although the religious people who survived did not necessarily support the armed insurrection of the guerrillas, they had come to share much of the Marxist analysis of Central American history and opposed the rule of the oligarchs in those terms. The six Jesuits priests who were murdered by the Salvadoran Army in late 1989 were actually campaigning for an end to the war, for although they sympathized with the leftist revolutionaries, they felt that the ongoing war supported by the United States would only continue to destroy the Salvadoran countryside and the people themselves. It was their insistence that the Army and the oligarchs had to compromise with the rebels and begin sharing power with the vast majority of Salvadorans that angered the right-wingers.

As the decade of the 1990s began, it appeared that the Salvadoran government, despite its vast military assistance from the United States, could not defeat the guerrillas militarily and would seek some kind of compromise. As terrible as the social devastation has been during the past ten years of well-publicized warfare, there was an even greater loss of life elsewhere in Central America. In Guatemala, a leader in the export of death squads and extreme right-wing ideology, even more people have died than in El Salvador. The Guatemalan era of repression and death has been enforced for almost forty years, an experiment in the "anti-communist model" which has produced only misery.

Chapter 8

ONE RED BANANA CAN SPOIL THE WHOLE BUNCH

In 1954, the United Fruit Company, the largest landowner in Central America, had a problem: the government of Guatemala was buying unused agricultural land and giving it to poor peasants.

The United Fruit Company could count on the United States government:

John Foster Dulles, Secretary of State, was the former lawyer for United Fruit on Wall Street.

Allen Dulles, Director of the CIA, had written the contracts for United Fruit with Guatemalan dictators.

John Moors Cabot, Secretary of State for InterAmerican Affairs, was brother of the president of United Fruit.

Robert Cutler, National Security Advisor, was former chief of United Fruit's main bank.

Henry Cabot Lodge, U.S. Senator from Massachusetts and later Ambassador to the United Nations, was a large shareholder in United Fruit.

Ann Whitman, President Eisenhower's secretary, was wife of the public relations director of United Fruit.

The United States decided to sponsor a military coup that overthrew the moderately left-leaning, democratic government of Guatemala.

Guatemalans have lived in a right-wing state of terror ever since.

ONE RED BANANA CAN SPOIL THE BUNCH

It was one of those moments when a powerful capitalist government really acted like a "committee of the bourgeoisie." The United Fruit Company was an important client of the U.S. government because its interests in Central America were substantial:

- 3,000,000 acres of land (565,000 acres in Guatemala, 91% of it unused)
- 2,000 miles of railroads to carry bananas to port
- 100 steamships to carry bananas to North America and Europe

The United States removed the Arbenz government with a CIA plot that simultaneously destabilized the Guatemalan economy, planted blatant disinformation in the international press, and armed and organized an invasion force in neighboring Honduras. Since the U.S. coup was successful it became the model for future destabilization of various governments by the CIA, a model that was followed almost to the letter in the 1980s in the effort to overthrow the Sandinista government in Nicaragua.

The United States, in its support of the steady profitability of U.S. business interests, has mounted numerous invasions of Central American and Caribbean countries in the twentieth century, but none was more unfortunate than the 1954 subversion of Guatemalan democracy. Just as in the 1953 CIA plot that overthrew a democratic government in Iran on behalf of U.S. oil companies, the CIA action in Guatemala doomed a country and a region to decades of repressive and murderous rule under dictatorial regimes.

Before the U.S. intervention, from 1944 to 1954, Guatemala had enjoyed the first truly democratic government in its history, one that was promoting steady economic growth and granting economic justice to the poor Indians and ladinos who made up the huge majority of the population. Like the rest of Central America, Guatemala had always been ruled by an oligarchy which seized the best agricultural lands for its own use and suppressed all efforts of peasants and workers to earn a fair living. This changed under the Arevelo and Arbenz governments of 1944–1954:

- one half of the nation's agricultural and industrial workers were organized into unions.
- 1,500,000 acres of land were distributed to 100,000 peasant farmers.
- literacy and access to health care were increased dramatically.

The progress was so impressive that the Guatemalan oligarchy failed in numerous attempts to topple the government, perhaps because they were no longer united in their efforts to oppress the poor. Some members of the oligarchy sympathized with the move toward democracy: President Arbenz himself had 1700 acres of land that were redistributed to the poor in 1953; his Foreign Minister Guillermo Toriello gave up 1200 acres at the same time.

LEADING GUATEMALA TO THE SLAUGHTER

With the overthrow of the Guatemalan government and the obliteration of its successful reforms, the United States announced that it would show how superior the U.S. version of free enterprise was to the Guatemalan experience under the so-called "Communism" of Arbenz:

> *"President Castillo Armas' objective, to do more for the people in two years than the Communists were able to do in ten years, is important. This is the first instance in history where a Communist government has been replaced by a free one. The whole world is watching to see which does the better job."*
> - Richard Nixon, 1954

Contrary to Nixon's predictions, the anti-communist alternative to the progressive democracy of Arevelo and Arbenz was not 2 years of impressive growth, but 35 years of military dictatorship. The country did not prosper. Extreme deprivation became the norm for Guatemalans, 86% of whom live in poverty today. Land distribution is even more unequal than in El Salvador or in Nicaragua before the 1979 Revolution. The Guatemalan upper classes, which collect so much of the income, enjoy the lowest taxes in Latin America. Consequently the education systems and health care systems are among the worst in the Hemisphere. Most people never finish even a third grade education and the infant mortality rate is higher than any other country except Haiti's.

Terror became the way in which the rich and the military maintained order. From the very beginning, when a U.S.-backed government was installed in 1955, democracy was the loser:

- Colonel Castillo Armas was rewarded for leading the military coup and named President in a very limited election.
- Land distributed to peasants was given back to large landlords.
- Labor leaders were rounded up, jailed, or executed.

33

Although U.S. money arrived, in the form of very generous foreign aid grants and business investment, most Guatemalans were unhappy with the return to rule by the oligarchy. A guerrilla war, aided by a dissident group which had left the Armed Forces, began a rebellion in 1960s which was only put down with the help of U.S. Green Beret soldiers. Resistance among the general populace continued to grow in spite of the initial defeat of the guerrillas; labor union strikes, mass student protests, church communities allied to the poor, and new guerrilla movements among the rural Indian population continued to grow throughout the 1970s and into the 1980s.

The response of the military-oligarchic alliance was brutal, and more deadly than the terror of any of the other brutal regimes that supported the agricultural export economy in Central America. Besides giving direct military assistance, the U.S. arranged to have military training and operations overseen by experts in the international terror network: Somoza's National Guard from Nicaragua; Israel's Security Forces; and the Army of Argentina, which was also busy "disappearing" its opponents at home. Well over 100,000 people, most of them peasants and Indians, were murdered or "disappeared."

In the years 1980 to 1983, the Guatemalan Terror, or "La Violencia," as it is still called, was claiming victims at an extraordinary rate. Often the advocates of peaceful change were the first to be exterminated by government death squads:

- In June 1980, 27 union leaders were abducted from the unions' confederation building in downtown Guatemala City. In August, 1980, 17 more union leaders were kidnapped while at a meeting in a Catholic retreat house. None ever appeared again.

- In 1980 and 1981, 20 Catholic priests and nuns were assassinated or kidnapped. Five Protestant ministers were murdered. 91 priests and 78 nuns left the country under threat of death. Hundreds of Catholic catechists, or lay workers, were murdered. Churches and church schools were burned and closed. Seventy Catholic parishes no longer had priests. In the province of Quiché, not a single Catholic church remained open.

The Guatemalan Army has been admired by the other repressive regimes in Central America for its ruthless efficiency, some of which is attributed to the expertise of its Israeli trainers. It could operate with even less impunity than other armies because one of its enemies was unique to Guatemala: the large indigenous population of Indians.

THE EXTERMINATION OF INDIANS

In most parts of Central or Latin America, the indigenous population was wiped out centuries ago or was left in tiny pockets isolated in the jungles or remote mountains. In El Salvador there are virtually no Indians and a huge majority of the population, like that in Mexico, consists of "mestizos" (called "ladinos" in Guatemala), brown-skinned people of mixed Spanish and Indian ancestry. Guatemala has a large ladino population which is generally subservient to the mostly white oligarchy; however, there are also various Mayan (or Indian) groups remaining, who make up at least 50% of the population, many of them inhabiting their own villages throughout the country.

These descendants of the Mayas fought a long and bitter war against the Spanish in the early 1500s and since then have mounted rebellions whenever the government and landowning gentry tried to push them out of their villages and communal fields. The introduction of coffee plantations to Guatemala in the 19th century renewed the exploitation of Indians. The plantation scheme had modern attributes and incorporated railroads and capital from German banks; although similar to the primitive capital accumulation initiated by Columbus, it was more efficient. The Indians were left in their villages and brutality was measured out more carefully so as not to decimate the valuable workforce.

As German settlers took over most of the coffee business, the Guatemalan government pushed the Indians off the fertile slopes and valleys below the volcanoes; it was eager to attract capitalist investment and "modernize" the country. New laws were passed to provide labor for the expanding plantations: in 1934 a male Indian who was working his own fields or engaging in some trade was declared a "vagrant" and subject to heavy punishments if he did not work 150 days of the year for the plantation owners. The pay was so poor that an Indian man could not possibly support his family; families were dependent on growing their own food on plots of land that only became smaller and smaller as they were pushed higher and higher into the mountains, often farming at altitudes of 8,000 to 10,000 feet.

As the twentieth century wore on, this kind of "modernization" and expansion of export agriculture kept increasing; more and more land was expropriated to grow bananas, cotton, and beef cattle, even vegetables for the supermarkets of North America. More labor was required at various times of the year: whole families of Indians were crammed into trucks in the highlands and driven down to the coastal plains where little children labored beside their parents for months at a time; they were poisoned by heavy use of pesticides and forced to live in unhealthy, disease-ridden camps.

Earlier in this century, when there were still few roads across Guatemala, Indian servants were forced to carry their white masters or mistresses on their backs as if they were beasts of burden; usually it was cheaper than using a donkey or a horse. This practice had been begun by the Spanish centuries earlier, and the new immigrant-investors were not adverse to engaging in the same kind of humiliation of the natives. As in all of the Americas, there was a need to invent and perpetuate racism when the white population was intent on severe oppression of a black or brown workforce.

A Catholic priest who helped Indian villagers build hundreds of their own schools in the the 1960s and 1970s (he was driven out of Guatemala by the military in the 1980s) recalled one visit by a provincial governor who was inspecting the education system but refused to believe that these "sub-humans" could learn.

> The governor asked his aides, *"Who taught these people to speak? What can these shriveled up oranges possibly think?"*

At this time, the Catholic Church in rural areas offered not just material help, but also a "liberating gospel." Poor ladinos and poor Indians were encouraged to look at their own lives through the social commentary of the Bible; while conservative churchmen in the cities were still congratulating the rich on their place in a social order ordained by God, their rural counterparts were giving the exploited spiritual encouragement to throw off their bonds. This occurred at the same time that separate large scale guerrilla movements, like the Guerrilla Army of the Poor and the Organization of the People in Arms, were organizing resistance to the military dictatorship among ladinos and Indians throughout Guatemala. As in El Salvador, people felt armed resistance was necessary because years of peaceful opposition had failed; campesino cooperatives, student movements, workers' unions, and political parties had been violently dispersed by the government and their leaders were routinely murdered.

The uprising of the poor gave the ruling alliance between the oligarchy and the military an excuse: "to complete a process that began in 1542: the acquisition of control over the countryside and the total breakdown of village autonomy," according to Jim Handy in his book *Gift of the Devil*. Claiming that they were fighting a holy war against "International Communism," the military under President Rios Montt, a convert to a U.S. fundamentalist church, proceeded to wage total war in the remote countryside. Because the guerrillas were elusive, the Army targeted non-combatants who were identified as guilty by their race and distinctive dress - massacres occurred in 440 Indian villages in the Northern and Western highlands. Hundreds of thousands of refugees fled to Mexico and the United States, while about a million were displaced to new locations within the country, like the shanty towns around Guatemala City. In a country where terror had been employed before, the level of violence reached new heights. The Guatemalan Bishop's conference reported in May of 1982:

> *"Not even the lives of old people, pregnant women, or innocent children were respected. Never in our history has it come to such grave extremes."*

By the mid 1980s the military had created "Development Poles" in many of the rebellious provinces; these were militarized villages based on the system of "strategic hamlets" that the United States had invented in Vietnam. The Indians became prisoners in fenced-in garrisons which featured loudspeakers and daily patriotic chants and prayers; they proceeded to and returned from their fields under armed guard. The countryside and the Indian life that had survived for centuries was being "rationalized" for the further expansion of the agro-export industry.

In 1985 the civilian President Cerezo was elected, but he conceded that he only held "30% of the power" while the Army controlled the balance. In desperate attempts at modernization, his government allowed tax free opportunities for foreign corporations to locate in Guatemala. The burgeoning metropolitan area in Guatemala City became a growing investment opportunity for American transnationals and their business partners among the local elite. One stretch of the Pan American Highway heading westward from Guatemala City is home to the new glassed-in offices and factories of 15 transnational pharmaceutical corporations, most of which make beauty aids and drugs; they appreciate the low wages and the "stability" which the regime is trying to supply.

By the late 1980s, the two major television stations were owned by Mexican investors and the Army ran its own TV network which features, among other things, Pat Robertson's 700 Club. There is also a Protestant evangelical channel which broadcasts the right-wing ideology of

Robertson and other U.S. preachers; it is primarily owned by investors in the United States.

Hundreds of U.S. businessmen operate in Guatemala, perhaps because they can expect, according to those interviewed by Allen Nairn, "at least a 30 to 35 percent return on equity." One North American investor was asked how he would respond to a labor leader who became active in his business:

> *"Shoot him or eliminate him. Assassinate him. Murder him. Whichever word is most applicable."*

Life under a terrorist government became barbaric in the 1980s and 1990s. Today, in spite of the extreme repression, the guerrilla forces are making a comeback amid poverty and social dislocation that is worse than ever. The Army, in which corruption is rampant, seems unable to successfully engage them in combat. Compromise gestures by the military toward the insurgents seem unlikely because the U.S.-approved "anti-communist" culture is too well established. In short, the framework of pro-capitalist state terrorism probably cannot be dismantled without an appropriate signal from the North.

Chapter 9

NICARAGUA: TRYING TO ESCAPE THE GRINGO

1855 - William Walker, a wayward gringo from Tennesee, invaded Nicaragua with an armed band, briefly made himself President, and tried to introduce African-American slavery.

1907-1933 - The United States invaded Nicaragua repeatedly with U.S. Marine forces. Augusto Sandino, a dedicated nationalist, led a guerrilla army that forced the Marines to depart.

1936 - After killing Sandino, Anastasio Somoza, a soldier trained in the United States, established a thoroughly corrupt dictatorship which lasted 43 years.

1979 - A popular revolt, led by leftist nationalists calling themselves Sandinistas, pushed the Somozas out of Nicaragua.

1981 - President Ronald Reagan, who saw the Communist menace everywhere, feared that the Sandinistas were the tool which the Soviet Union would use to take over the rest of Central America, Mexico, and his ranch in California. With the help of another wayward gringo, Colonel Oliver North, Reagan embarked upon various wild and illegal schemes, including the Contra War, in order to destroy the Nicaraguan economy and overthrow the Sandinistas.

NICARAGUA: TRYING TO ESCAPE THE GRINGO

William Walker began the pattern of U.S. adventurism in Central America in 1855 when he landed in Nicaragua leading his Phalanx of Immortals, a band of 58 roguish characters he had recruited on the docks of San Francisco. He offered his services to the Liberal Party and helped their army unseat the ruling Conservatives in a very brief war. Then he proceeded to overthrow the Liberal leaders and name himself President of Nicaragua; in one of his first declarations he legalized slavery.

Generally, U.S. public opinion, both in Congress and in the media, supported Walker. Northern magazines like *Harper's Weekly* praised his "resolute heroism" because it promised the extension of the glory of the U.S. empire; Southern newspapers like the *Richmond Enquirer* appreciated Walker's intention to make Nicaragua into a new state, an extension of the U.S. South. By extending Southern slavery to Nicaragua and introducing African labor, Walker felt conditions would be ripe to permit the full flowering of gentile plantation civilization. He wrote:

> *"The conservatism of slavery... goes to the vital relations of capital toward labor, and by the firm footing it gives the former it enables the intellect of society to push boldly forward in the pursuit of new forms of civilization."*

Walker's racist theories of economic development led him to believe that Latin America was cursed by the confusion of trying to exploit the labor of a population in which Indian and White races had mixed. Nicaragua, he thought, would be rescued by a clear white/black demarcation of master and slave:

> *"With the negro-slave as his companion the white man would become fixed to the soil; and they together would destroy the power of the mixed race which is the bane of the country."*

Walker also pleaded for the understanding of capitalists in the United States, for he felt that "capital in its battle to master labor" needed the extra weight of slavery; otherwise the free laborers of the North would overwhelm capital at the ballot box with "free democracy."

As it turns out, capitalists paid no attention to his theories, but did want to use him for their own purposes. Two enterprising financiers, Garrison and Morgan, had schemed to send Walker to Nicaragua in the first place because they wanted to take over the highly profitable business of the Accessory Transit Company, owned by the first great North American tycoon, or "robber baron," Cornelius Vanderbilt. The Transit Company transported many thousands of people on the fastest route from the East Coast of the United States to the Gold Rush in California. Vanderbilt paid the government of Nicaragua $10,000 a year in order to bring huge profits home to the United States. By legal agreement, he was supposed to share a tidy portion of these profits with the Nicaraguans, but the clever "Commodore" Vanderbilt employed a trick still used to great effect by transnational corporations today. He kept an extra set of accounting books which showed that Accessory Transit made no profits at all, but sustained a loss instead, and refused to pay the Nicaraguans a penny more than the paltry $10,000 annual fee.

When William Walker declared himself President of Nicaragua, Vanderbilt and his managers in Nicaragua seemed to like the idea. But when President Walker proceeded on a course of turning over the Transit business to Garrison and Morgan, Vanderbilt was furious. He brought a large lawsuit against his small-time rivals in the United States and ordered his Central American employees to encourage opposition to Walker's blatant invasion of Nicaragua. The governments of the other Central American countries, emboldened by these developments, mustered a joint army together and drove Walker out of Nicaragua in 1857.

Walker, forever the grandiose dreamer, returned two years later without the backing of U.S. financiers; he was promptly captured in Honduras in 1860 and executed.

THE ERA OF THE SOMOZAS

In the early part of the 20th century the United States found that its repeated invasions and occupations of Nicaragua, from 1907 to 1933, were futile, especially after an ardent nationalist named Augusto Sandino raised a tenacious guerrilla army in the mountains. Then Washington decided to rely on an easier method of controlling a Central American government. Anastasio Somoza, who had been trained in the United States, was the commander of the National Guard which had, in turn, been created by the U.S. Marines. Somoza offered a truce to the rebel General Sandino, because Sandino and his army had successfully driven the U.S. Marines out of the country and inflicted repeated defeats upon Somoza's National Guard. After a dinner which celebrated the peace talks, Somoza arranged to have Sandino assassinated. Within two years he was able to name himself President of Nicaragua, a job he kept for life.

The Somoza family rule was continued by his son, Tacho, and lasted for 43 years. The family proceeded to become the nation's largest landholder and controlled about 20% of the Nicaraguan economy. As elsewhere in Central America, access to the international agro-export economy became very profitable for the nation's oligarchy of rich families. The Somozas were particularly corrupt in their manipulation of property and foreign aid, but did not succeed in supplanting other elite families who resented their crude ways. When a popular uprising of Marxist guerrillas, student rebels, and angry campesinos emerged in the 1970s under the banner of the nationalist Sandinista Front for the Liberation of Nicaragua, there were many sympathizers among the middle and upper classes.

The Somozas could not hide the corrupt nature of their business dealings, which became most obvious after the 1972 earthquake that leveled much of the capital city of Managua. Rather than use the large amounts of international relief funds to rebuild the city, the Somoza family channeled it into their own projects or used it to bribe government functionaries. The United States government seldom wanted to investigate the corruption and misery perpetrated in Nicaragua because the Somozas were first class anti-Communists. When Guatemala needed to train their military to contain popular discontent after the 1954 U.S.-sponsored coup, the Somozas provided their National Guard to do the job. When John F. Kennedy and the CIA wanted to prepare the Bay of Pigs army for the invasion of Cuba in 1961, the Somozas offered a secret training site in Nicaragua.

Fred Sherwood, a U.S. businessman in Guatemala and former head of the U.S. Chamber of Commerce there, appreciated the Somozas dedication to the U.S. point of view. Tacho Somoza once proclaimed to Sherwood, "You tell me tomorrow, 'Tacho, kill all the Communists.' And I'd go out and kill them."

In the 1960s and 1970s the land holdings of the Somozas and other elite landowners expanded exponentially. Cotton and sugar plantations as well as cattle ranches produced exports for the U.S. and world markets. Thousands and thousands of peasants were pushed off their own small farms to make room for the plantations and ranches, so that poverty increased dramatically even as export earnings were producing an economic boom for the rich. During a twenty year period the meat exports from Central America tripled and helped fuel the growing meat consumption in the United States,
which increased by 50% per capita. Central Americans, rather than benefiting from the increased production of beef cattle, saw their meat consumption fall by 30% per capita.

IN WITH SANDINISTAS

In the mid 1970s, while small bands of Sandinista guerrillas roamed the mountains and occasionally harassed the National Guard, a new breed of Catholic priest was preaching to the poor campesinos in the Nicaraguan countryside. They brought the message of the Vatican Council of 1961–1965 and the Medellin Conference of 1968: the poor had a right to stand up for themselves; the Gospel preached social redemption as well as promising rewards in heaven. The Jesuits created the Educational Center for Agrarian Advancement, which not only searched for ways that small farmers could become more productive but also told them that they had a right to keep their land, or reclaim land that had been unjustly expropriated from them.

As the Church prepared many rural Christians in base communities to become lay workers who could spread this social gospel, the peasants became more confident of their ability to organize and defy the authority that the Church had formerly conferred on the rich landowners and the military. Many church workers became political activists as well; like their Jesuit teachers, they found themselves joining with the Sandinista Front members to organize Committees of Agricultural Workers.

When the Sandinista rebellion swelled from a guerrilla movement to a full-fledged revolution supported by people throughout the cities and countryside, the United States was hardly prepared to deal with the situation. In the last month of warfare, when Somoza started heavy "revenge bombings" of the residential neighborhoods of his own cities, the U.S. State Department stopped promising its support. When Somoza was quickly ousted and spirited out of the country to join other former right-wing dictators in exile, the U.S. seemed to expect that the Nicaraguan landed gentry, the old oligarchy, would be prepared to take over. The Sandinista leadership informed Washington that this was not the case, that this had been a people's revolution of all classes. (Indeed, many of the young Sandinista leaders were children of the middle and upper classes who had been radicalized in the 1960s just like their contemporaries in the United States and Europe.)

The United States was not prepared to deal with a wide-ranging left coalition of Marxists, liberation preachers, peasant activists and middle class reformers. It looked like Communism to Ronald Reagan, just like Guatemala in 1954. The U.S. used all the tricks that it had used against Guatemala, plus the kind of CIA-directed economic sabotage it had practiced in Chile in 1973. It also created a large, well-armed Contra army in Honduras, largely made up of the National Guard troops who had left Nicaragua after the Revolution. (Had the Sandinistas, in their moment of victory, been too magnanimous, since they neither executed nor imprisoned most of this notorious security force?) The Contras forced the Nicaraguans into a full-scale mobilization for war, which ultimately drained more than 50% of government revenues, funds that were desperately needed elsewhere.

In spite of severe hardship, the Nicaraguans managed to create a vastly improved health delivery system and a literacy program that reached into the nation's smallest hamlets. During the years from 1980 to 1983, before the most severe U.S. economic sanctions were imposed, the Nicaraguan economy was the only one in the region that showed positive growth. Still, some early revolutionary initiatives were recognized as serious mistakes and corrected. Most of Somoza's lands, up to 20% of the farmland in the country, were converted to large, inefficient state farms; after a few years many were divided up and added to the lands that were redistributed for direct ownership by cooperatives and individual campesinos.

Another, more criminal mistake, was the harassment of the Miskito Indians on the isolated Atlantic Coast. These English speakers, descendants of escaped black slaves from the Caribbean, were discriminated against by the Spanish speaking Nicaraguans from the populous Western regions. Although the CIA temporarily recruited a few Miskitos to join the Contra effort, the Nicaraguan Government later reached an accord with them, apologizing for its conduct and offering local autonomy to the Miskitos.

The survival of the Sandinistas throughout the 1980s was remarkable given that the United States supported a brutal war against revolutionaries in El Salvador, tacitly backed the "Violencia" committed against the people of Guatemala by their government, made a military colony out of Honduras, and invaded nearby nations like Panama and Grenada. One reason the Nicaraguan Revolution lasted for eleven years was the unique role played by progressive religious forces. Although much of the Church hierarchy was consulting regularly with the CIA and the U.S. State Department, the people's church gave sustenance to those who defied the established economic and cultural order of the past 500 years in America.

Finally, in the spring of 1990, the Sandinistas could no longer survive the barrage of economic, political, and military sabotage directed by Washington. Conservative Violeta Chamorro won the Presidential elections and unseated the Sandinista leader, Daniel Ortega, in large part because people of all classes were anxious for an end to the violence and the economic deprivation. Many Nicaraguans hoped that a flood of economic aid would flow down from the colossus of the North and nourish new growth and prosperity, but this was not the case. By 1992 the promises of free market capitalism had proven to be empty, and the life of the average citizen was more wretched than before.

Whatever the faults of the Sandinista leadership, it was clear that the United States deserved the most credit for the failures of the Revolution. The Nicaraguans, not the North Americans, had clung to principles of democracy and resisted the temptation to impose the kind of internal state terrorism which is so acceptable in Guatemala and El Salvador. For this reason, the ideas of equality and liberation are still alive and the Revolution may yet be resurrected in some new form.

Chapter 10

LIBERATION FROM THE STRUCTURES OF POVERTY AND OPPRESSION

"But many who are first shall be last; and the last shall be first."

-Matthew 19:30

In Latin America, and in many other parts of the world where the majority is poor, the people have developed a theology of liberation. The poor are undertaking their own religious quest for equality and justice and spiritual understanding.

Most of these Christians would tend to agree with the Nicaraguan textile worker who said:

"They say we are Marxists, or that we are mixing Marxism and Christianity. Really, we do not know anything about this Marxism. We have never read Marx in my barrio, or in the base community. All we know is what we read in the Bible. It is the source of our Christianity and of our politics."

In some parts of Latin America, being associated with an active "base community" of believers can invite violent retribution from government death squads. Religion was once used to make the rich feel secure, but now the message of Jesus inspires great fear among the ruling elite:

"It is easier for a camel to go through the eye of a needle than for a rich man to enter the kingdom of God."

-Luke 18:25

"For the oppression of the poor, for the sign of the needy, now will I arise."

- Psalms 12:5

LIBERATION FROM THE STRUCTURES OF POVERTY AND OPPRESSION

Liberation theology has developed since the 1960s, first within the Catholic Church, then within some Protestant denominations. Religious people witnessed the struggle of socialists and Marxists, revolutionaries and reformers, in the fight against poverty, social injustice and government tyranny. It occurred to the religious that the revolutionaries, even if they rejected the Church as an outdated crutch of the oligarchical elite, were often doing the work of Jesus: fighting oppression of the body and spirit, and martyring themselves on behalf of the poor.

At the same time, a remarkable change had taken place within the Catholic Church worldwide with the convening of the Vatican II Council of 1961–1965. The Church, under the direction of Pope John XXIII, committed itself to a democratic renewal by opening up many new paths of free expression among the Church hierarchy and the lay believers; even more important, it embarked on a serious effort to make social justice a central component of Christian life. It declared a "preferential option for the poor," an identification with the Church of the early Christians and their practice of primitive communism:

> *"And all that believed together, had all things in common. And sold their possessions and goods, and parted them to all men, as every man had need."*
>
> Acts 2: 44–45

The Catholic option for the poor did not signal an outright rejection of the rich, who had curried special favor with the church ever since it allied itself with the Empire of Rome under Constantine, but it did mean that the poor of the world were to receive special attention. The physical needs of the poor - food, housing, employment, education, and material security - were to be met first; then spiritual attention could be given to everyone. When the Dogmatic Constitution was rewritten at Vatican II, it proclaimed that the institutional Church was not supposed to build up its own treasures:

> The Church *"is not set up to seek earthly glory, but to proclaim humility and self-sacrifice, even by her own example."*

At the same time that the Church was transforming itself with Vatican II, a Catholic theologian in Peru, Gustavo Gutierrez, was writing about a theology which offered the poor a chance to liberate themselves from the oppressive structures of the world economy, from the neo-colonialism of the U.S. and Europe:

> *"The basis for his analysis was not Marxist revolution but the Exodus and Christ's Good News to the poor of the freedom from oppression."*

By 1968, the Bishops of Latin America had absorbed enough of Gutierrez' ideas to suggest a new definition of "sin" which coincided with the social analysis of Marx and other revolutionary thinkers. The bishops said that the most serious sin in Latin America was the "social sin" of "institutionalized violence," that is, the physical deprivation of the majority at the hands of the oligarchy of the rich and the threat of military brutality and terror toward those who would question this arrangement of society. The Bishops noted that "institutionalized sin" had begun with the systematic war which the Europeans had waged against the Indians for centuries; it had evolved into a structural exploitation of the large majority of Latin Americans, an exploitation so extreme that it amounted to "class warfare" of the rich against the poor.

In response to this institutionalized class warfare waged by the rich, most liberation theologians rejected the violent reaction of many Marxists; that is, they did not choose to fight back in this class war by joining an armed revolutionary movement. The new theology did not propose passivity in the face of evil, however; it advocated active non-violent resistance to class oppression.

A CHRISTIAN REVOLUTION

At the heart of this rapid transformation of Catholicism were thousands of priests and nuns and millions of poor peasants and poor workers organized into over 300,000 "Christian base communities" in the countryside and city slums of Latin America. These groups emphasized the formation of close, caring communities of believers who study the Bible, discuss the teachings of Jesus, and apply those lessons to their daily life. In such democratic settings, the priests lived among the poor as teachers, a far cry from the distant authority of clerics in ornate cathedrals. Poor people discussed the teaching of Jesus - the story of the Good Samaritan, the encounter with the young man who was told to give away his riches - and reflected upon the prophetic vision of the Old Testament God who fought on behalf of the oppressed. They reached liberating conclusions: that they were entitled to love and dignity in this world and that "the meek" could truly "inherit the earth."

42

These communities empowered the people: they formed agricultural cooperatives, pressured landlords to relinquish unused land, organized with unions of factory workers and agricultural workers, demanded civil rights, fought for health care and schools in their poor barrios and hamlets. There was often violent response from the owners of property and the armed forces. By the end of the 1970s over 850 priests and nuns had been martyred throughout the Americas, killed for their identification with the poor. But the murder of these church workers was selective, an attempt to frighten them out of their new loyalties. Far more widespread was the murder of church lay workers and the general population of believers. People who were practicing non-violent resistance were being wiped out by the terror tactics of the elite opposition. Some priests had to ask themselves a very difficult question; were they leading their followers to the slaughter?

Father Ernesto Cardenal, later to become the Minister of Culture in Nicaragua, lived in a spiritual community called Solentiname on an isolated island in the middle of Lake Nicaragua. There, in the early 1970s, poor peasants lived alongside young students, some of whom who had fled the materialistic life of the city. Not only did the people gathered at Solentiname share the fruits of their labors in the fields, but they also engaged in the spirited production of art, especially painting and poetry. At that time, throughout Nicaragua, many Delegates of the Word, lay Catholic teachers who formed congregations when there were no priests available, were being tortured and "disappeared" by the National Guard. Then the Guard attacked the community of Solentiname and murdered a number of members. The inhabitants reflected upon the violence that was being unleashed - perhaps it was necessary for the people to fight back. Furthermore, to some it seemed necessary to go beyond a socialist analysis of society, which progressive Christians were already adopting, and actively join the Marxist revolutionaries. Father Cardenal decided that it was not enough to engage in the Christian-Marxist dialogue that many adherents of liberation theology advocated; he declared himself a Marxist Christian and joined the Sandinista Liberation Front.

THE OPPOSITION

Liberation theology and revolution are, of course, anathema to the ruling elites in Latin America and the United States. Their powers of retribution in a particular country may be so great that an armed rebellion by a Christian-Marxist alliance may invite horrendous reprisals and bloodshed. What is the solution in El Salvador, for instance? The six Jesuit priests who were murdered in December of 1989 were forcefully calling on the the government and the rebels to lay down their arms and reach some kind of compromise political solution. They were slaughtered by agents of the Salvadoran military, who were content to let the war drag on indefinitely as long as they were supported by U.S. dollars.

In Nicaragua, the widespread rebellion of the people came under great opposition pressure from the Catholic Church itself. Although the Sandinistas may have occasionally brought the opprobrium of a conservative Catholic hierarchy upon themselves by their own hubris and insensitivity, there was a more important factor. Although liberation theology is valued in many parts of the Latin American Church and has even found its admirers and adherents in the U.S. Church, the Catholic Church hierarchy is still organized in Rome under an authoritarian system led by Pope John Paul II. As Penny Lernoux, author of *People of God*, pointed out:

> "The reforms spawned by Vatican II have not gone unchallenged, however. Since 1978 when John Paul II became pope, a counterreformation, known as the Restoration, has been in progress."

The Pope has attempted to maintain discipline over a worldwide Church that seeks democratic renewal within its own structure and progressive change within the world's political economy. In his attempt to stem the tide the Pope has fought with the Bishops of Brazil over liberation theology, as well as with nuns and priests of the United States over sexual matters and the freedom of women; Vatican councils have censored theologians and the books produced by various Catholic orders in many countries. Such is the conservatism of the Pope, so foreign to the change emanating from Vatican II, that he was rather easily enticed into an anti-communist alliance with the United States. Although he claims to be against political activism in general, he has encouraged the activity of right-wing religious groups like Opus Dei and the Knights of Malta.

Ronald Reagan's Ambassador and influential member of the Knights of Malta, Vernon Walters, met with the Pope in 1983 to discuss the Nicaraguan situation and to suggest that some stern measures be taken by the Vatican. John Paul II responded by demanding that four Sandinista priests resign from their top-level government positions or leave the Church. Even more telling was his personal animosity when he travelled to Central America in 1983 and visited Nicaragua. Upon arriving he refused to let Father Ernesto Cardenal, who kneeled before him, engage in the customary show of respect to the Pope - kissing the Pope's hand and Papal ring.

Later the Pope appeared before 700,000 of the Catholic faithful in the main square in Managua, where the giant crowd hoped to hear the Pope bless all the people who had died fighting the Contras. When the Pope refused to acknowledge these losses and engaged in a stern lecture to the Nicaraguan people, the crowd chanted, "We want peace! We want peace!"

The Pope, unable to contain his anger, simply screamed into his microphone:

"Silencio! Silencio!"

But there was little effect, and little respect for the Pontiff.

Chapter 11

COUP DE GRACE: FUNDAMENTALIST AMERICANISM, AN EVANGELICAL COUNTER-REFORMATION

"He is putting down wrong-doers and punishing those who are evil doers...Let it be an example of what God can do when His people are in charge."

- Pat Robertson describing General Rios Montt's bloody dictatorship in Guatemala, 1982

While great ferment arose within the Catholic Church throughout the 1980s, right-wing TV evangelists like Pat Robertson and Jimmy Swaggart were running amok in Central America (with the open encouragement of the U.S. government.)

Fifteen years of intensive Protestant evangelization was changing the face of Latin America. On the one hand, there was a flood of conservative missionaries and dollars from fundamentalist churches in the United States; on the other, there was the remarkable growth of indigenous churches amid the disintegration of the old economic and social structures of the Hemisphere.

Evangelical Protestant Church Membership (as a percentage of the population)

Guatemala - 34%	Nicaragua - 20%
Chile - 25%	Brazil - 20%

COUP DE GRACE: FUNDAMENTALIST AMERICANISM, AN EVANGELICAL COUNTER-REFORMATION

In recent years the Catholics have lost their religious monopoly in Central and South America. In 1990 Pat Robertson, the right-wing preacher who wanted to be President of the United States in 1988, created a media opportunity for himself to take credit for the religious transformation of Central America. Robertson arrived in Guatemala City to launch Proyecto Luz, or "Project Light," a six month campaign to convert two million people throughout Central America (one million of them in Guatemala) to evangelical Protestant Christianity. The effort began with three one hour TV programs prepared in Spanish by the Christian Broadcasting Network for showing on all TV stations at 8 p.m. primetime; 60% of the televisions in Guatemala, which are now found in shanty towns and Indian villages as well as middle class homes, were tuned to the first show.

Very soon Guatemala will boast the first Protestant majority of any country in Latin America. If Robertson's Proyecto Luz had delivered the coup de grace and reached its goal of one million instant converts in 1990, then about 50% of the country would already be evangelical Protestants. In fact, if only regularly practicing believers were counted, Guatemala probably had more Protestants than Catholics even before Robertson's arrival.

Pat Robertson, of course, does not deserve credit for this amazing transformation of culture over a few years time, for it was a complex mixture of exterior pressure and interior desperation that helped bring about this religious shift. It has been spurred on by a decade of terror and disaster: fierce warfare, massive social dislocation, and economic ruin have been the rule. Terrorized people were searching for a haven amidst the social chaos. Many Catholic priests and Protestant pastors who provided help to the poor and encouraged social reform were forced to flee from countries like Guatemala, El Salvador, and Honduras because their lives were threatened. Thus a spiritual vacancy existed for the conservative fundamentalists to fill.

It is worth remembering that the Religious Right in the United States, and Pat Robertson in particular, had a major role to play in bringing war and economic ruin to Central America. He was not just a preacher to the Contra army but a major fundraiser as well; he was a constant friend to the brutal Salvadoran military and the economic oligarchy which stands behind it; he coordinated a massive program of "humanitarian aid," called "Operation Lovelift," to the Guatemalan Army in 1982-1983 at a time when it was committing its most blatant massacres in hundreds of villages in the Western Highlands. Over the years Robertson has enjoyed the help of fanatical right-wingers: Senator Jesse Helms and born-again Ollie North, General Singlaub of the World Anti-communist League, and the evangelical General Rios Montt of Guatemala were just a few of his cohorts. There has been a strange and frightening fusion of right-wing elements: U.S. fundamentalists, privileged Latin oligarchs, neo-fascist military elites, and roving anti-Communist vigilantes of both North American and Latin American origin. The right-wing fundamentalist versions of U.S. culture, education, economics, and political philosophy have become the predominant ideological exports from the United States to many countries. Certainly this speaks of the power of the conquistadors-this is not new in world history - to impose their religious and cultural values upon the vanquished. The direct adoption of U.S. religious norms is most evident within the newest churches which administer to the needs of the more comfortable citizens. In these congregations, prosperous believers are most conscious of emulating or mimicking the North American models of success and they find the neo-Pentecostal or charismatic version of fundamentalism, the kind that Robertson sells, most congenial.

However, these upper-middle class churches which buy into the political and social message of the Religious Right represent a distinct minority of Protestants in Latin America. Most Protestant churches are in the older Pentecostal tradition that preaches deliverance from sin, ill health, and alcohol to the poorest citizens. They are conservative in their prescriptions of strict personal behavior and exuberant in their celebrations, offering loud and long services with episodes of faith healing and speaking in tongues. They offer people at the margins of society, and others who are being pushed down to a threadbare existence, a straight and narrow path that allows for survival. Also, their spirited services offer welcome emotional and physical release to people who are exhausted from working and scavenging unceasingly the rest of the week.

These Pentecostal churches, so popular among the extremely poor of Guatemala, Brazil, and many other countries, have little interest in the right-wing political message from the U.S. Many of their denominations are home-grown and require no training for pastors beyond a calling from the Lord. Perhaps they are apolitical because being politically active is a dangerous practice which disturbs the repressive authorities; most new congregations are content with surviving amidst the rapid disintegration of their societies. For many, the Catholicism that bound them to their local communities was part of a larger pattern of life that has been shattered by economic uncertainty and dislocation. A small Protestant church is particularly attractive to those who have been displaced to a new part of the country or who are struggling to make a living at a new occupation outside of the traditional networks of their village, barrio, or old extended family.

The neo-Pentecostal churches serving the higher classes have a much more highly developed sense of conservative political ideology. The rich and those aspiring to be rich are looking for some understanding of why their economies are so fragile, not to mention some moral justification for the fact that they enjoy good fortune while others starve. Their pastors teach a distinctly North American brand of "prosperity theology," sometimes called the "name it and claim it" school, because they believe the Lord is standing ready to answer one's prayers for wealth. In their Christian schools, Satanism is directly equated with Marxism and principals and teachers are quick to note that "secular humanism" is not allowed to poison the minds of their children. Finally, in churches like El Verbo in Guatemala, the home church of General Rios Montt, the solution to the nation's ills are preached repeatedly: "discipline, discipline" and when that fails, "more discipline." The church steadily preached the second coming of Rios Montt as God's chosen leader of Guatemala, something that almost came true in the 1990 elections.

When Pat Robertson descended from the U.S. to have television chats with Rios Montt in the Spring of 1990, this helped the ex-dictator become the leading candidate for the presidential elections held later in the year. The General was forced to withdraw because of a law that does not permit ex-dictators to run for political office; however, the wide variety of evangelicals who supported Rios Montt easily transferred their energies to his evangelical cohort, Jorge Serrano, who had headed the civilian council which advised Rios Montt during his dictatorship in 1982–1983. Serrano was elected by a surprisingly large margin, winning 67% of the vote in the final two way race against a traditional conservative candidate. Guatemala, which only 20 years before had been 97% Catholic, had managed to elect an evangelical Protestant president.

RELIGIOUS HEGEMONY

Although war and repression and direct U.S. intervention are important to the evangelical Protestant boom, they are but part of a process which is wrenching poor, developing societies into fuller participation in the capitalist world. Just as Protestantism once played an important role in the growth of advanced capitalist countries like England, Holland, Germany, and the United States, now it seems poised to play its part in the expansion of capitalist cultural hegemony to many areas of the world. Within this context Pat Robertson is not just a rabid anti-Communist conspirator who cooks up schemes with the Ollie Norths of the world. The religious milieu in which he operates is real, that is, it has real power for the people who are indigenous to the developing countries and is not just the ephemeral creation of the North American spiritual developers.

The late twentieth century has been an era of fantastic religious ferment, when the worldwide Islamic fundamentalist movement is probably even more powerful than Christian fundamentalism, when strong localized revivals of conservative Jewish and Hindu minorities are shaping the futures of their countries. There are some observers who see the Islamic movements as demonstrating strong resistance to modernization, to the cultural hegemony that generally arrives with capitalist expansion; or, perhaps, as a groping attempt to work toward economic modernization without surrendering all Islamic values to the amoral offerings of corporate commodity culture.

Other observers, like the sociologist Peter Berger, think we are in the midst of a second Protestant Reformation through which Max Weber's Protestant Ethic can spread throughout the world. At his Institute for the Study of Economic Culture at Boston University, Berger has celebrated the coming of the "Second Protestant Internationale," a label that tries to suggest the "revolutionary" potential of Protestantism while ignoring the context of political repression within which it prospers.

A better interpretation would reject the idea of a new Reformation in favor of the idea that we are simply witnessing the spread of Protestant culture as capitalism continues to expand and deepen its roots in all parts of the world. From this point of view, a reactionary Protestant culture is now creating its own counter-Reformation in the face of real social reform as it is being developed by both Catholic and Protestant adherents of liberation theology.

In this era when the reality of a capitalist empire dominated by one power, the United States, must eventually give way to a more truly international capitalist order, there is also a need for a new cultural hegemony. The old social-religious hegemony of the Catholic Church in alliance with the ruling classes in Latin America has crumbled. This hierarchical and rigid social system, which had once been appropriate for the primitive accumulation of capital from plantations and mines, is no longer functional, thereby forcing many countries to attempt to impose capitalist order in the most brutal ways. A new religious hegemony cannot simply praise the ruthlessness of government authority; it must also offer social practices conducive to the accommodation of the lower classes. Thus we must examine the evidence that the new Christian "enthusiasm," especially on the part of conservative Pentecostal and neo-Pentecostal churches, is not only real, but somehow meets the real needs of people struggling to survive the social transformation of further capitalist development.

THE RELIGIOUS "METHOD"

A British sociologist of religion, David Martin, has guarded hopes (from a point of view that sympathizes with both Protestantism and capitalism) that the Evangelical revival sweeping through Latin America and some other repressive societies - South Korea, South Africa, and the Philippines, for instance - will somehow transform them into liberal, democratic societies in the future. He bases his hopes in part on the example of the Methodists in England at the beginning of the industrial revolution. Although his argument falters badly because he does not properly address the degree to which today's new evangelizing nations are suppressing democratic movements, he brings up the interesting parallel between today's burgeoning Pentecostals and the enthusiastic Methodists of 1750 to 1850 in Britain.

The worship of Methodists in their early days was spontaneous and loud, filled with enthusiastic singing and, so it seemed to the very proper Anglican upper class, with wild and irreligious expression. Early Methodism gave ample room for participation by workers and artisans who felt a direct calling from God and were ready to preach directly from the Good Book. Behavior expected of congregations was uncompromisely strict and demanded abstention from drinking, dancing, and all kinds of frivolous social behavior. Women, although not allowed into the highest leadership positions, were particularly drawn to Methodism because of its enthusiastic worship and the opportunities it afforded for engaging in all kinds of group activities. To reinforce their piety and strict observance of moral codes, believers met regularly in "cells," small discussion groups not unlike modern Bible study meetings in which people, generally segregated by sex, would discuss their personal failings and the "method" of conduct and thought which would cleanse their spirits.

Following the lead of its founder John Wesley, who had his first success preaching to 3000 impoverished miners in Bristol, early Methodism was the church of displaced rural people and the impoverished working class. The value of money and absolute thrift were emphasized greatly; since the first hundred years of the Industrial Revolution in England meant a lower standard of living (if not pauperization) for most of the working class, the strict moral code of the Methodists led them to waste not a penny nor a moment of time, thus increasing their chances to escape to some upper level of the lower classes. At the same time, the Methodists engaged in various kinds of self-help and adult education, usually of a distinct kind which would help members advance in the Church and, perhaps, to a job like foreman in a factory.

All these traits can be found in the Pentecostal sects which are now proliferating around the world, including the tendency to center the whole family's life around various church activities on every day of the week. From the harsh demands of working long hours at very low pay, people are granted enthusiastic and joyful release on Sundays and evenings. As a way to escape from slums, crime, and the social disintegration that characterizes the mass migration of the poor to the cities, the believers willingly submit themselves to the strictest narrow path of behavior under the "shepherding" of their authoritarian pastors. Over the long haul, perhaps more than a generation, many Protestants notice practical results: they get ahead at work and keep their families intact.

These kinds of Protestants, keeping their noses to the grindstone without complaint, are welcomed by the property-owning elite, because they not only make dependable employees and small traders, but also tend toward political quietism. In England, the early Methodist ministers openly opposed political and trade union organization for their members in order that the Anglican authorities would not interfere with the rapid growth of their church. An early Methodist leader, Richard Wilberforce, put the message in clearly subservient class terms:

"practical Christianity [that is, Methodism]
makes the inequalities of the social state
less galling to the lower orders... reminding

*them that their more lowly path has been
allotted to them by the hand of God."*

English historian E.P. Thompson has described
the felicitous cooperation between upper and lower
classes that was promoted by the new religious
formations around 1800:

> *"They fostered within the Methodist church
> those elements most suited to make up the
> psychic component of work-discipline of
> which the manufacturers stood most in
> need.... it is exactly at this time that
> Methodism obtained its greatest success in
> serving simultaneously as the religion of the
> industrial bourgeoisie and wide sections of
> the proletariat."*

The emergence of alternative religious practice,
removed from the controlling interactions with the
old ecclesiastical hierarchies, also amounted to an
escape for the new working classes from the crushing cruelties of the new economic system. Their
religion was not just "the opium of the people," but
was also (to quote Marx further) the "heart of a
heartless world" and "the sigh of the oppressed."
On the other hand, the whole process of creating
new religion, particularly as more and more sects
were formed, offered new opportunities for working
class members to take leadership positions and
develop a talent for public speaking.

For instance, in 1812, the Primitive Methodists
broke away from the Methodists with a congregation of 200 people; by 1850 they had 104,762 members. The original leaders of the Church were
"Hugh Bourne, a humble carpenter, and William
Clowes, a working potter." They incorporated
much of the Methodist system, but they also featured some of the important practices that characterize present-day Pentecostals around the world:
speaking in tongues and faith healing. Their unin-
telligable shouting in church and their loud
proselytizing on the street earned them the nick-
name of the "Ranters."

In spite of their emphasis on individual piety
and the magical use of "gifts of the spirit," a number of Ranters became involved in labor organizing, where their powerful preaching style earned
the attention of other workers. In the big coal strike
at Durham in 1844, the coal manager for the Earl
of Durham complained that:

> *"There is a class of self-sufficient leaders,
> who are generally local preachers, and who
> are decidedly the most difficult to control,
> and who urge others to acts of very great
> insubordination."*

The Wesleyan Methodists, in contrast, were
politically conservative and their preachers
regularly gave sermons admonishing their congregations to steer clear of both unions and
workers' political organizations. John Wesley
seemed convinced that his job as spiritual leader
was to build up the fortitude of individuals, not a
class of people, who could thereby achieve mobility
into the higher classes - thus proving the efficacy
of the Methodist "method." It was not until after
1850 that Methodist preachers dropped their opposition to working class political associations. At
that time a "social gospel" started to develop within
Methodism, and Methodist Sunday schools are said
to have contributed to the education of a number of
progressive political leaders.

THE CENTRAL AMERICAN METHOD

The parallels between the British and Central
American experiences with evangelical Protestantism, both of which seem to be integral with
capitalist development, are limited and must be
expected to diverge in the long run. The example of
the rapid growth of Methodism in Britain is worth
noting because it indicates a little bit of the com-
plexity of religious culture evolving under
capitalist hegemony. Thus, we ought to note that
even though the ideas of the North American
Religious Right, Pat Robertson, and the neo-Pentecostal churches seem important in their role as
the vanguard of capitalist culture, perhaps their
ideology could be turned upside down by some un-
foreseen developments within the indigenous churches and the rapidly changing working class
culture of Latin America.

Within the neo-Pentecostal movement in
Guatemala and other countries, the upper classes
are being drawn into their own anti-intellectual,
semi-fascistic brand of Protestantism. It is built on
the U.S. model of consumer gratification and justification of wealth and does not seem likely to
spawn the "non-conformist" culture that allowed
intellectual invention at other times in Protestant
history (especially among the English Puritans,
but also amid English and North American Protestants of the 19th century.) Quite the opposite seems
the case; the new Evangelicalism is providing a
relatively painless way for the middle and upper
classes to conform to the international values of
commodity capitalism while jettisoning a wornout
version of aristocratic Latin Catholicism (since
they are quite unlikely to adopt a new Catholicism
of liberation which challenges their right to monop-
olize prosperity and property.) The countries of
Latin America are obviously not in the position of
Great Britain in 1750, on the verge of establishing

a world empire and becoming the leader of industrial capitalism at the same time. Although the British exacted a terrible toll of misery upon their working class for one hundred years, eventually the profits of industrialization and the profits of empire combined to raise the standard of living of all classes considerably and helped defuse the revolutionary ambitions of the wage earners.

The countries that make up the majority of America, then, are unlikely to escape their positions on the bottom rungs of the capitalist world system, where they are constantly being stepped on. It is by no means likely that in four or five generations they will arrive at bourgeois democracy for all amid capitalist prosperity. More likely will be the need for constant doses of repression to keep them in their subservient positions within the international order. Such long-term repression does, and will, require a cultural hegemony which teaches "discipline" and "respect for authority" among all classes, while justifying God's rewards for those at the top of the local social structure. It is not a pretty picture, any more than it was at the beginning of the industrial revolution:

> *"the proverbial Non-Conformist mill owners, with their Methodist overlookers, and their invidious reputation as weekday child drivers, work[ed] their mills till five minutes before midnight on the Saturday and enforc[ed] the attendance of their children at Sunday school on the Sabbath."*
> - E.P. Thompson, *The Making of the English Working Class*

Part III

Chapter 12

CAPITALIST DEVELOPMENT

"The overwhelming proportion of the world's work-forces, who live in rural zones or move between them and urban slums, are worse off than their ancestors five hundred years ago."

-Immanuel Wallerstein, *Historical Capitalism*

It is worth recalling that the original industrial revolution in Britain was a brutal affair:

In the 1790s the great landlords and gentry of England controlled 80% to 85% of the land. 40% of the peasants had been forced off the land. The misery of the new mill towns awaited them.

In 1844 in Liverpool, one fifth of the working class, or 39,000 people, lived in 7,800 damp and dirty cellars without ventilation or sewage facilities.

In 1842 Parliament's Report on the Employment of Children revealed that many coal mining employees were children under the age of 13, some as young as 4. They worked at least 11 hours a day and often more than 14.

CAPITALIST DEVELOPMENT

We jumped from the early years of European imperialism in America to the present day situation in Central America in order to demonstrate that the process of conquest is still proceeding. The harsh logic of unfettered profit-taking reigns supreme, not because of something peculiar to "Spanish" culture but because of the constant demands of the world capitalist system on the weaker countries. Where repressive force can be properly deployed, then extra surplus value will be extracted in both agro-export industries and manufacturing assembly production.

Although the Central American countries may be exceptional, and exceptionally unlucky, in their proximity to the United States and because of the levels of violence that have persisted there for decades, the rest of Latin America and the Caribbean are also suffering at the hands of the world economic order. Greater and greater proportions of their economies are being forced to conform to the expectations of the world market and the regimen of late 20th century capitalist life. The adjustments required are detrimental to most people's lives, but as we are reminded by the few facts on the previous page, this is nothing new. Capitalist development requires exploitation.

The process of capitalist modernization, which drives poor people off the land and into even more impoverished circumstances in large urban areas, occurs all over the world now. In their struggle for survival, vast numbers of unemployed people compete for a limited number of low wage jobs. To those in the advanced countries, the social disaster often appears in appeals for charity: magazine readers in the U.S. are persuaded to send a few dollars a month to support the little Latin American girl who is pictured in the advertisement as she picks through the garbage dump, looking for clothes or the next meal. But few of these same readers would stop to think that this girl is a typical victim of capitalism, perhaps no worse off than her English predecessor:

The Job of "Hurrying"

In the first half of the 19th century, the job of "hurrying" in the British coal mines was performed by half-naked girls, aged 6 to 21, who pulled coal wagons out of the mines by a chain that went between their legs as they crept along on their hands and feet.

This kind of dehumanization, marketed today under the name of economic development, is being resisted by a great many people. American history has taught them - that is, five hundred years of emerging capitalist relations have made evident-that exploitation produces profits, but never for themselves and seldom for their own countries.

By the end of the 19th century the great wealth accumulated by Britain, not just from the great new productivity of its industrial empire but also from its worldwide military and mercantile empire, finally allowed its working class to enjoy significant increases in its standard of living. In the other advanced industrial nations of Europe and North America, a similar result transpired as the 20th century began. This was not a gift from capitalists whose generosity knew no bounds, but instead was the result of constant struggle by working class organizations and unions in tandem with their progressive allies. They used strikes and struggled through parliamentary and democratic processes to alleviate the terrible working conditions that capital had created. The success of these struggles, which were interrupted repeatedly by wars and depressions, was also dependent upon the existence of the huge amount of wealth amassed by the capitalist classes, so that a liberal solution of sharing a small portion of the wealth - rather than a revolutionary solution of changing the system-was the end result (or the temporary balancing mechanism) achieved by the class struggle.

But the partial progress of the working classes in the industrialized countries is not necessarily permanent; nor does it represent a path to a better standard of living that can be followed by wage laborers throughout the world. Immanuel Wallerstein has reached a rather controversial conclusion about historical capitalism: that Karl Marx was right when he predicted the absolute immiseration of the working classes. Many Western intellectuals, especially at the moment of rejoicing over the "victory" of capitalism over communism, look at the relative prosperity of the working classes in a few nations of the world, and therefore think Marx's notion of an oppressed working class was ridiculous, that it did not account for the great productivity of capitalism. Wallerstein, however, looks at the worldwide capitalist system, 500 years old, and sees what Marx saw throughout England in the early 19th century - a grim reality for working class people around the world:

"Greater human immiseration in the global context - for 10 or 15 per cent of the people in the world capitalist system consume more than they actually produce and have seen rising standards of living - the other 85 per cent lives in poverty. The gap between the

52

15% and the 85% has been getting greater for a long time."

In Latin America, and most of the world for that matter, it is difficult to imagine how there will ever be a build-up of bourgeois wealth which spills over into the lower classes. First of all, today's leading capitalist countries have had the opportunities to prey upon the raw materials and mineral wealth of the rest of world and organize its agricultural production for plantation export. Such imperialism, either in its old guise or in the newer version of neo-colonialism which operates through transnational corporations and banks and the national elites which cooperate with them, does not seem to offer possibilities for the "developing" or "emerging" nations. Not only do these emerging nations lack the capital extracted from other nations, but they seldom get to hold onto the capital generated in their own economies.

By calling attention to the parallels between the first capitalist development in England and the current wholesale rush (a forced rush, to be sure) of Latin America and the other parts of the world into fuller participation in the capitalist system, we can note that several things happen almost simultaneously in emergent industrial capitalism. These are general social/political/economic phenomena that seem to be repeated at each stage at which new countries are brought into the modern class system of industrial production.

1. There is "enclosure," methods for pushing people off the land. Landowners, first the local or planter elite, later agro-corporations, remove the peasants from their ancestral lands and "rationalize" production, introducing innovations which produce greater yield (yield in terms of profit, not necessarily in terms of food) in the national and international markets.

2. The displaced rural people flock to the towns and metropolises looking for work or seeking survival by begging or theft. There is great vagrancy in rural areas, too, with concurrent large scale increases in crime. Accordingly, punishments often become more severe in a futile effort to deter crime.

3. There is general impoverishment - a huge mass of underemployed people are willing to accept work for incredibly low wages, for many hours per day, to eke out their survival.

4. There is an epidemic of ill health because so many people do not have the means for proper food and sanitation; such things as rickets and tuberculosis became prevalent in 19th century England; other maladies like typhoid and oral dehydration from chronic diarrhea have afflicted the Third World today.

5. Paradoxically, there are great increases in population even though this population is becoming ever more unhealthy. English population doubled between 1800 and 1850. The population of the developing and under-developed nations has increased from about 2.7 billion to about 3.8 billion from 1965 to 1988.

6. Because capital is concentrated in very few hands, once it is accumulated it lies begging to be regenerated by new capitalist activities. New factories are built to take advantage of the overabundant labor supply and the quantity of surplus value that can be exploited from the new class of wage laborers.

7. Quite aware of their oppression and the difficulty of simply surviving, working people fight back for higher wages and better living conditions. They risk their livelihoods and their lives in struggles to form unions and political parties. Sometimes they think about owning and operating the industries themselves; that is, they consider some kind of alternative to capitalist control of their lives; they think about "socialism," or social constraints that can be put upon money and private ownership.

8. The owning classes respond with coercion or violence - in 1799 England banned political organizations and unions for workers; organizers could be arrested. In the 1980s, similar tactics have been used, from Korea to Central America; if anything, methods are harsher today - in Guatemala and El Salvador the ruling elite often choose to simply exterminate union and peasant leaders, rather than put them in jail.

9. Some members of oppressed classes seek solace in new religious forms, like Methodism in 18th and 19th century England, and Pentacostalism in 20th century Latin America. Others look to social organization and politics - the Chartists and the cooperative movement in England; leftist political parties and revolutionary movements in Latin America. A promising, and subversive, kind of religion for the emerging working classes today is liberation theology, because it attempts to construct a new religious experience that can merge with a class-conscious model of social and political participation.

GREAT LEAP FORWARD?

By drawing on the comparisons between early industrial England and late 20th century Latin America, we are simply conveying the idea that there are certain continuities in the patterns of capitalist development. We now proceed to examine the course of the conquest of the Americas in the 19th and 20th centuries, the neo-colonial era in which individual countries played distinct roles in the industrial revolution or in the expansion of European and North American control over world markets. During this time, the processes of industrial revolution and social revolution have been interacting continuously to produce the structures of inequality that bind the American nations to the capitalist world system of the present.

During the 18th and 19th centuries, the Spanish empire faded from the world scene and so did its peculiar relationship with the early capitalists of Europe, the banks and mercantile houses outside of Spain that had prospered from the Spanish (and Portuguese) imposition of forced labor in the Americas. Gradually Spain's control over its colonies deteriorated, and so did the value of plantation exploitation for England and France in the Caribbean. As the English capitalists increased their fortunes and their new Empire increased its reach, followed by similar developments in the United States, the next stages of capitalist development were often dictated by the deployment of money belonging to these two leaders of the world system. Thus, as the various countries of America became ostensibly independent in political terms in the early 19th century, they soon found themselves extremely dependent upon the whims and investments of the capitalist powers, including the new one directly to the North.

At this point it is necessary to stress once again that the United States is not "America" but just one part of America. During the first half of the history of the Europeanized America, the lands that make up the U.S. and Canada were of very minor importance. If during the last 200 years these places achieved a dominant role, it was not because the United States is typical of America. Its development was unique, so that a combination of favorable circumstances and actions led to the growth of a powerful capitalist economy and the presence of some truly democratic institutions.

Accordingly, the U.S. has been an anomaly, the part of America where capitalism and European imperialism brought something more than social disaster. But this is not to suggest that the United States escaped the evils of capitalism; many people had to pay the price for its rapid economic expansion.

Chapter 13

NOT THE LAND OF THE FREE,
NOT THE HOME OF THE BRAVE

1789 - The U.S. Congress made one of it first promises:

"Utmost good faith shall always be observed towards the property of the Indians; their land and property shall never be taken from them without their consent."

1829 - After years of Indian Wars promoted by such men as Andrew Jackson, the 7th U.S. President, the Cherokees and the Creeks and the Choctaw were removed from the Southeast and pushed all the way to the western side of the Mississippi.

1890 - Wounded Knee, South Dakota: the U.S. Army massacred 300 Indians -men, women, and children.

"It was the climax to four hundred years of violence that began with Columbus, establishing that this continent belonged to white men."

- Howard Zinn, *A People's History of the United States*

Theodore Roosevelt expressed the sentiment of most white people:

"I don't go so far as to think that the only good Indian is a dead Indian, but I believe nine out of ten are, and I shouldn't inquire too closely into the case of the tenth."

NOT THE LAND OF THE FREE, NOT THE HOME OF THE BRAVE

The development of industrial capitalism in the 19th century was incredibly dynamic and productive, as well as amoral and avaricious. In Europe, for all the wealth produced, and the freedom and leisure that this wealth allowed the bourgeoisie and the middle class (perhaps 10% of the population at most), the early years of capitalist expansion were a period of immiseration for the working classes and peasants who labored incessantly. In the United States, the situation was somewhat different: millions of square miles of the most fertile land on earth had been taken from the Indians and were available for farming.

"America" - usually meaning the United States- was overly idealized as the land with streets of gold by the Europeans, but it certainly offered rewards to many immigrants. If they could survive the hard life of the homesteader, they could become free farmers who operated amid an expanding continent-wide agricultural market controlled by railroads and commodity traders in Chicago and New York. The economy was expanding so rapidly - in monetary terms, in geographical sweep across the continent, and in population - that there were constant opportunities for some energetic immigrants to leave the urban bleakness behind and establish their own small businesses and farms in towns sprouting across the U.S.

First, of course, the land had to be cleared - not of trees, but of inhabitants. The Indians signed hundreds, if not thousands of treaties with the U.S. state and federal governments. All of them were really temporary holding measures on the part of whites who wanted to be granted the use of Indian lands. After a short period the treaties were broken by white settlers, investors or the U.S. Army, then war was made again and new concessions were demanded from the Indians.

The same pattern of warfare and removal that decimated the tribes east of the Mississippi proceeded to eliminate the major tribes of the West, too - the Sioux, the Utes, the Cheyenne, and all the others - until the United States was free for what the preachers and politicians called its "Manifest Destiny," the ability to expand from the Atlantic Ocean all the way to the Pacific, the completion of God's sacred plan. In the process the population of original Americans was decimated:

North American Indian Population
1492 - over 7,000,000	1900 - 350,000

The North American Indians were uncooperative; they had not allowed themselves to be enslaved or forced into indentured labor. Only briefly had they allowed themselves to be pulled into the production of huge profits for the Europeans and that was through the practice of one of their traditional skills, trapping animals. The Indians did not realize it, but their dealings with the Dutch, English, and French traders would eventually serve to nearly wipe out one of their fellow inhabitants in the North American forests: the beaver.

This was a seventeenth century example of an environmental disaster perpetrated by a forerunner of the transnational corporation, the Dutch West Indies Company. Since a flurry of fashion throughout Europe demanded "beaver hats," which were covered with the fine underfur, "fur wool," of the beaver, the Dutch traders came to control most North American fur trade at the same time they were monopolizing the Eastern fur trade with Russia. In one of the early examples of "corporate" integration of production worldwide, the Company took the American furs to Russia, where they were processed along with the beavers and other fur animals captured on the Russian frontiers. Then they transported the semi-finished product through their Baltic shipping lanes to all of Europe where they were generally able to control distribution and price.

The near extermination of the beaver also served inadvertently as the means of decimating the Indian population, which suffered great epidemics of smallpox and other European diseases which were transported in part by the fur traders. Another change, just as damaging to the culture of the Indians, was that the original Americans increased their competition for a scarcer and scarcer beaver population. The result was, says anthropologist Eric Wolf, that:

> "The fur trade thus changed the character of warfare among Amerind populations and increased its intensity and scope."

The inability of the Europeans to enslave the North American Indians or even hire them for a wage had presented a problem. How to develop all this "free" land? The logical economic answer, after removing the Indians from the land, was the slave plantation system.

> "The developmental problem was one of bringing into production tracts of land available for the asking, or little more, but in the absence of an adequate labor supply... free labor would not do... since the land was free."

> "The slave plantation, producing some basic commodity for the mother country, was a special, emergent form of industrial organization."

> - anthropologist Sidney W. Mintz

THE LAND OF THE NOT-SO-FREE

1502 - The first African slaves were brought to America.

1863 - Slavery was abolished in the United States.

1965 - The Civil Rights Act put an end to 100 years of Jim Crow laws, strict segregation, and very overt discrimination.

1981 - President Ronald Reagan and his Attorney General Edwin Meese decided that African Americans had been spoiled by "reverse discrimination." Economic and social life for people of color deteriorated very quickly and there was a resurgence of racism throughout the land.

From these dates we can compute the African-American scorecard in the Western Hemisphere and the United States:

1502 to 1863:	361 years of slavery
1863 to 1965:	102 years of severe discrimination
1965 to 1980:	15 years of some improvement in social and economic conditions
1980 to 1992:	12 years of renewed racism and economic decline

---

THE LAND OF THE NOT-SO-FREE

We ought not to forget how much of the wealth that fueled the growth of the United States came from the slave labor of the African Americans. For instance, in the first half of the 19th century, the Indian Wars removed the original Americans from Southeastern U.S. so that huge expanses of virgin land could be planted in cotton. Between 1815 and 1860 this one crop produced by slaves comprised over one half of the United States' export profits. Of course, other slave products boosted the agro-export total even higher - tobacco from Virginia, rice and indigo from South Carolina, and sugar from Louisiana.

The exploitation of the African Americans did not rest simply upon a system of oppression of black-skinned people by whites, but was intensified by a class system characterized by extreme differentiation in wealth and status among whites themselves. The plantation elite lived an elegant, spendthrift existence at the expense of everyone else. The 1850 Census of the United States showed the following about life in the Southern states:

The Good Ol' Days

- 1000 white plantation families received $50,000,000 in income (about $50,000 per family per year.)

- The other 660,000 white families received $60,000,000 in income (less than $100 per family per year).

Plantation life was a capital-intensive agro-export kind of farming, really an agro-industry. Large fortunes or large loans had to be expended to purchase the slaves and set up the operation. But the returns were quite remarkable, even before the advent of cotton production. James Madison, the fourth President of the United States, bragged to an English visitor about the astounding productivity of his slaves in Virginia shortly after the American Revolution:

Madison earned $257 from the labor of each African American each year while only spending $12 to $13 on maintenance, feeding, and housing.

After the slave trade with Africa was ended in 1808, raising and trading slaves within the United States became more and more profitable. States like Virginia became the slave "growers" while the new plantation states like Mississippi became the slave "importers." Between 1850 and 1860, 269,287 slaves were exported from the Atlantic states to the Western states at the very lucrative price of about $1000 apiece. One of the cruelties often perpetrated upon the slaves by their white masters, the prohibition of marriage, was really an exigency necessary to meet market conditions. A seller of slaves had to be able to separate men, women, and children, whether related by blood or not, at a moment's notice in order to meet the needs of the buyer. Otherwise, if the families had been sold together, their price might have been unnecessarily deflated.

The treatment of slaves in the United States, that is, their physical care, was somewhat better than in the Caribbean. Some scholars like Eugene Genovese attribute this to the unwritten codes of behavior developed among plantation owners, who formed a sort of "pre-capitalist" aristocracy which sometimes valued honor over maximum profit-taking. These owners, unlike their counterparts in the Caribbean who were usually absentees living in England, often lived in the mansion within sight of the shacks of the slaves. Of course, this better treatment can also be attributed to the end of the slave trade in 1808, meaning that the expanded market in slaves could be met by encouraging a natural increase in the African-American population which would occur only if the slaves were treated well enough to reproduce and maintain certain kinship relationships.

Carter Godwin Woodson, in *The Negro in Our History*, recognized that some slaves were treated slightly better by some masters, but that such treatment declined as whole expeditions of whites and their slaves left the Atlantic South to create new plantations of cotton and sugar in Mississippi, Alabama, Louisiana, and Texas. There, the new production was tied into the industrialization of capitalism. U.S. cotton, two thirds of all cotton grown throughout the world, was shipped to the factories of England (and later, to New England and the Mid-Atlantic states) where new machinery made cloth faster and faster; the introduction of cotton gin machinery greatly increased the productive capacities of the plantation, a kind of agricultural factory. Sugar production was being reorganized, too, as steam powered mills increased the amount of acreage that could be processed. Inventions such as the complex "evaporating pan," patented by a free African American in Louisiana named Norbert Rilleaux, greatly increased the efficiency of the refining process.

Concern with high production often increased the oppression of the slaves, especially on absentee-owned plantations where overseers received a proportion of the profits for the year. The overseers, like their counterparts in the Caribbean, often mistreated slaves, ultimately killing them, in order to produce short-term profits. Because they received a share of these short-term gains, they did not necessarily care about the longer term use and viability of the slaves any more than they would have worried about taking care of valuable machinery. (In the Caribbean in the last years of slavery, 1808 to 1834, the planters attempted to make life a little easier for their slaves, who "only" worked 90 to 96 hours per week and had Sundays off as well as two days at Christmas; the planters also began to censure fellow owners or overseers who beat their slaves to death. Still, the conditions remained bad enough that the population declined because replacements no longer were available from African shipments.)

The biggest expansion of U.S. slavery and the plantation system came in the second quarter of the 19th century and was due to the rapid growth of the cotton manufacturing industry. At the same time, sympathy with the slaves and interest in the abolition of slavery decreased markedly in the Southern and border states because slavery was the basis of the new economic boom. Southern churchmen began writing learned documents which bolstered pseudo-scientific arguments of racial inferiority with Biblical pronouncements which justified human servitude. The "curse of Canaan," refer-ences to the black "descendents of Ham," and admonitions such as "Servants, obey your masters" seemed sufficient evidence that God wanted the African American to be owned by the European American. The religious acceptance of slavery became so widespread that even the Methodist Church, which had grown very rapidly in the United States and originated with strong anti-slavery views, felt pressured into changing its tune. In 1836 the Methodists issued a clear disavowal of their former position:

The Methodist Church did not have "any right, wish, or intention to interfere in the civil and political relation between master and slave, as it existed in the slaveholding states of the union."

Ultimately the system of slavery died during the American Civil War, a victim of the primacy of wage labor over slave labor in the development of industrial capitalism. "Wage slavery" was not a kindly system either. Today it is especially cruel for the African American and Latin American workers who are locked into the bottom of the labor market by discriminatory practices. 150 years ago, when U.S. industrialization began, most white factory workers in the North lived a wretched existence, too.

Chapter 14

U.S. INDUSTRIALIZATION - NOT A PICNIC

1835 - New Hampshire: the workers in twenty textile mills - 1500 men, women, and children - went on strike. They lost the fight to establish a union but won a settlement for a shorter working day:
 Old hours: 13.5 per day, six days a week
 New hours: 12 per day, 9 on Saturdays

1860 - 20,000 shoemakers in New England went on strike to protest falling wages and rising food prices. Men earned $3 per week, women $1 per week for a six day, 90 hour work week. Women carried signs saying:

 "American Ladies Will Not Be Slaves"

1892 - 3,800 steelworkers went on strike at Andrew Carnegie's plant in Pittsburgh. The State Militia, armed with machine guns, subdued the striking workers. The steelworkers' union didn't return for many years.

1914 - The Ludlow Massacre. At John D. Rockefeller's Colorado Iron and Fuel Corporation, 11,000 Greek, Italian, and Serbian miners went on strike to protest falling wages. The State National Guard set fire to their tent colony, killing 11 children and 2 women.

1938 - The Hilo Massacre in Hawaii. Longshoremen tried to organize a multiracial union of pineapple and sugar workers. 50 union supporters were shot down by police.

U.S. INDUSTRIALIZATION - NOT A PICNIC

Working people in the United States spent one hundred years in constant struggle to form industrial unions. Only in the late 1930s, after a massive wave of sit-down strikes in the rubber industry and the auto industry, was widespread collective bargaining allowed. After social security and labor freedoms were instituted, American wages increased during World War II and helped provide a growing standard of living for the average U.S. worker in the 1950s, '60s, and early '70s. By the mid 1970s wages were starting to decline; from 1973 to 1991 weekly earnings had fallen by 19%. By the time of the "Reagan Revolution" of the 1980s, a conservative backlash by capitalists was in full swing; they succeeded in taking many social benefits and protections away from the working class in a crude attempt to increase profitability. Looking historically, the "good life" of the average American worker (of course, tens of millions of low-wage workers were still poor) lasted only about 30 years, a time coinciding with the benefits which the United States derived from being the leading industrial and military power in the world.

The recent rapid deterioration of working class life in the United States, which has hit people of color the hardest, has been distinctly "American." That is, compared to Europe, which also suffered from recession and the "sluggishness" of capitalism in the late 1970s and early 1980s, the U.S. provided very poorly for its working class population; it was ruthless in a way that the organizers of enterprises have always been ruthless throughout the Americas. As the standard of living of 80% of U.S. citizens was falling in the 1980s, the media was celebrating the increasing wealth and concentration of ownership among the upper class. The corporate media tended to remind the government to protect private property before protecting people, just as they had done at other times in U.S. history. In 1914 the reaction of *The New York Times* to the terrible deaths at Ludlow contained no sympathy for murdered workers, who were called "savage-minded men;" it spoke instead for the Rockefellers and all the other worried capitalists:

"With the deadliest weapons of civilization in the hands of savage minded men, there can be no telling to what lengths the war in Colorado will go unless it is quelled by force. The President should turn his attention from Mexico long enough to take stern measures in Colorado."

The early struggles of U.S. workers against the tyranny of the "free" wage labor system during the period of industrialization ought to remind us that the plight of poor white workers has at times been only marginally better than black workers. Workers in the shoe factories of New England in 19th century, working 90 or 96 hours per week, suffered from physical exhaustion almost as complete as the black slaves working at the time in the sugar plantations in the Caribbean. The hardships in the early New England factories were not so different from those endured by the first white laborers in North America. Indentured servants in North America were forced, or impressed, into the employ of the typical early Virginia plantation which, according to a recent Smithsonian Museum exhibit, was "best characterized as a corn- and tobacco-producing factory."

In 1624, at one thriving plantation called Flowerdew Hundred, there were 60 people working, 48 indentured servants and 12 free tenants and craftsmen. Of the 48 servants, 11 were black African workers sold into bondage by Dutch traders. There does not seem to have been much distinction between the conditions of labor forced upon the white and black indentured workers-things were quite deadly for all: between 1622 and 1625 plantation records show that 31 people died. This harsh environment for subjugated labor produced extraordinary profits from tobacco exports to England; just seven years after the founding of Flowerdew, the family investment group led by George Yeardley realized a huge profit on the sale of the property to another investor. When Yeardley died three years later he was the richest man in Virginia.

The plantation system of production, always tied to its European markets and centers of finance, would thrive throughout most of the 17th century by exploiting the "white labor" of indentured servants and tenant farmers. By 1700, the shortage of labor for the expanding system and the difficulty engendered by freeing the white labor force after some years of service led to the substitution of African slave labor. Radical scholars have argued about whether this early exploitation was truly "capitalist" or not. Orthodox Marxists would say that because it was not wage labor tied to the almost magical productivity of machinery, the plantation system was "pre-capitalist." Others, more allied to the looser definitions of Wallerstein and Braudel, point out that American plantations were a development of early capitalism that was particularly dependent upon the extraction of surplus labor from slaves, and thus was distinct from purely mercantile activity, the age old method of realizing profits by "buying cheap and selling dear."

This early agro-export capitalism, dependent on the European centers of finance, was experimenting with new forms of forced labor and organization for the precise purpose of producing a handsome return on venture capital. Although exploitative "free wage labor" was at first impractical in the New World, because of the plenitude of land and the shortage of labor, the early plantations provided lessons in the organization and coercion of labor that would be invaluable to those who would later conceptualize new forms of profit-taking by concentrating their labor forces in manufacturing centers. And, of course, the planters' fortunes, as they paid off large loans to the Northern banks, would ultimately build up the capital needed to invest in the machinery, coal extraction, and railroads that characterized the industrial revolution.

In the early 1800s, profits in manufacturing were created by a new system of exploiting labor in the industrial North. Since there was a continuous influx of immigrants and a growing number of farmers being pushed off marginally productive lands in New England, there was for the first time an abundance of cheap white labor in North America. "Free labor" did mean some freedom for white workers; they could choose to flee the oppressive conditions of the factory if they thought they could survive somewhere else within the economy or on the expanding frontier. "Free labor" also meant that the employer had new freedoms: to increase or decrease wages at a moment's notice or to dismiss as many of the workforce as were made superfluous by falling market conditions or increased mechanization; to have no responsibility for keeping people alive who the week before had been struggling to survive on wages at a bare subsistence level.

The adaptability of the new system of exploiting labor power was far superior to the slave system and allowed the owners to invest their fortunes freely in the exploitation of new developments in coal- and water-powered machinery. One of the severe restraints of slave labor was that one had to pay for a life-time of human work before it was transformed into marketable products. With wage labor huge amounts of investment capital were freed up for the development of technology, and only a portion of capital had to be reserved for labor; even then labor was paid for at the end of the week, not before the work started.

THE PECULIAR SITUATION OF THE U.S. WORKING CLASS

The brief notations of dates and strikes and repression at the beginning of the chapter ought to remind us that workers in the United States fought militantly for the right to form unions over a long period of time. What is paradoxical is that after this mighty battle, U.S. working class organizations and political parties have not had the same success in sustaining the powerful long-term presence that they have achieved in most of Europe. There, a working class political culture has forced more equal distribution of income and wealth and the adoption of social programs ranging from free health care to intensive employment training to liberal childcare leave.

In contrast to the European experience, it is worth mentioning some of special conditions in the United States that undermined long-term political solidarity among the working class:

1. Racism, which allowed white workers to see themselves as superior to African Americans and brown-skinned Hispanics, often made existing gulfs between skilled and unskilled labor, between industrial and farm labor, very much wider. A huge reservoir of low paid and unemployed people of color allowed employers to threaten their white employees with replacement by cheaper labor. Often the whites refused to consider the possibility of organizing themselves with their "inferiors."

2. Such prejudice carried over to other white immigrants, too, who were disdained by whites born in America for their foreign accents, customs, and racial characteristics. The steady and gigantic influx of immigrants over a period of one hundred years allowed employers to substitute fresh workers for those who had already become restive under the system. (Gavin Wright estimates that "In 1910 the foreign born and sons of the foreign born were more than 60% of the machine operatives in the country, and more than 2/3 of the laborers in mining and manufacturing.") Skilled, native-born workers were likely to isolate themselves in craft unions rather than organize themselves with the culturally distinct newcomers.

3. The extremely rapid population growth from immigration was matched by unparalleled room for expanding U.S. society towards the Western frontiers. This gave outlets to the discontented in two ways. First, the growing country needed ever more people at the middling level (storekeepers, accountants, and independent artisans of one kind or another) so that some of the energies of an oppressed working class were

drained upwards, so to speak. Secondly, there was room for both native born and immigrant to trudge West and produce for themselves on rich farming and grazing lands. The Homestead Act of 1862 provided an unprecedented opportunity for people without land to become self-supportive:

- 50 million acres of Western land were given free to families who would work on 160 acre farms for five years.

Of course, the politicians did not neglect the needs of the corporations, even in their infancy:

- 100 million acres were given free of charge to the railroad companies by the Federal government.

4. U.S. Protestant religion, in its multitudinous forms, was a formidable ally of the U.S. capitalist class. Various denominations had particular class positions to promote; for instance, Presbyterians and Congregationalists were quite resourceful in congratulating their middle and upper class WASP members on their successful achievement of material well-being, true proof of their "elect" status before God. Methodists and Baptists, who were the "non-conformist" minority in England, became the majority among Protestants with their "enthusiastic" religion of the masses. All of them recognized the sanctity of business and the special mission of "Manifest Destiny" as the United States kept expanding its frontiers and markets across the continent. (In regard to religious/cultural/industrial interactions, it is worth reading Anthony Wallace's *Rockdale*, a historical anthropological study of an early 1800s cotton industry town outside of Philadelphia. As more and more immigrants, many of them Irish, were brought into work at the expanding mills in Rockdale, the DuPonts and other important industry owners in the area actively promoted new evangelical churches which would preach humble submission and industrious habits to the these rough new workers. The increase in the new religious enthusiasm ran parallel to the decrease in the influence of the Mechanics' Society of Philadelphia, founded by Ben Franklin, and other secular organizations that had promoted self-education and egalitarian notions among the skilled working class.)

AFTER THE DEPRESSION

In the 1930s the simultaneous expansion of U.S. frontiers and business had come to an end and the harsh economic conditions of the Great Depression prodded working class people to create the great industrial unions of the CIO and then coordinate their activities with the craft unions of the AFL. Social security and work relief were created as government programs which were based on wide, universal coverage.

Laboring people of various ethnic backgrounds began to work towards common goals of working class dignity and material welfare. The growing industrial unionism culminated in the great wave of sitdown strikes in 1936-1937. 10,000 rubber workers in Akron, Ohio occupied their factories and refused to leave in 1936; scab workers could not be transported in and the corporations were afraid to attack the striking workers because their machinery might have been damaged in the process. The rubber workers' actions completely shut down the large tire manufacturers, Goodyear and Firestone, and culminated in the recognition of the union. Their success encouraged emulation in many industries:

1936 - there were 48 sitdown strikes in the U.S.
1937 - there were 477 sitdown strikes.
1937-1937 - In Flint, Michigan, the "Great Sitdown Strike" hit the core of U.S. manufacturing, the auto industry. 2,000 workers occupied General Motors' Fisher Body Shop #2. 5,000 more, carrying arms, marched in picket lines around the plant. The National Guard was sent in to quell the disturbance, but soldiers refused to fire on workers. The strike spread to other General Motors plants and the union, the United Auto Workers, was soon recognized.

By the time that World War II ended in 1945, almost all U.S. manufacturing and mining industries had been organized by unions. Many leftist union leaders and members were harassed during the anti-Communist "McCarthyism" hysteria that followed the war, but 34% of U.S. workers were organized and stayed loyal to their unions; they enjoyed a steadily rising standard of living throughout the 1950s and 1960s and were the only working people in the world who could afford automobiles, single family houses, and a college education for their children.

Various forces have undermined the security of workers since then: corporate anti-labor offensives, government hostility, and the ultra-cheap labor utilized by transnational corporations in developing countries. For the four factors mentioned earlier, and a host of other reasons, working class solidarity and unionism were weaker than in Europe. When assaulted by corporate economic weapons and upper class political pressure, the strength of U.S. unions eroded quickly:

In 1990 only 16% of U.S. workers were unionized.

Chapter 15

NEW WAYS OF EXPLOITING AMERICA IN THE 19TH AND 20TH CENTURIES

The advent of industrial capitalism expanded the opportunities for the North to dominate the rest of the world. The new capitalist powers, first Britain and then the United States, found ways to control the destinies of potentially rich countries throughout the Americas.

1890, Chile - Great Britain owned all nitrate mining, which produced 50% of Chile's total income.

1901, Cuba - Three years after the Spanish American War, U.S. corporations enjoyed almost total control of Cuba's economic assets: sugar, lumber, mining, cattle, tobacco, and railroads.

1911, Mexico - U.S. companies controlled 77% of Mexican mineral exports.

1920, Chile - Copper was the dominant export and the U.S. had purchased the entire industry.

"With adequate profit, capital is very bold. A certain 10 percent will ensure its employment elsewhere; 20 percent will produce eagerness; 50 percent positive audacity; 100 percent will make it ready to trample on all human laws; 300 percent, and there is not a crime which it will not scruple, nor a risk it will not run, even to the chance of its owner being hanged."

- Karl Marx

NEW WAYS OF EXPLOITING AMERICA IN THE 19TH AND 20TH CENTURIES

19th century neo-colonial dominance by the world's industrial powers replaced the system of outright plunder and enslavement that had characterized "Western culture" in America for centuries. The control of advanced capitalism may have appeared more humane than primitive capitalism, since the advanced state of business relationships and diplomacy did not require direct colonial rule; corrupting generals, bribing government officials, and buying up newspaper publishers were far cheaper. The new system managed to effectively deprive the countries of the South of their raw materials and capital, as well as any reasonable chance to share in the fruits of industrial development.

The unequal terms of exchange between the industrialized countries and the rest of the world are not chance encounters between those who want to borrow money and those want to earn a little interest on their savings. They are part of the long-term heritage of neo-colonial relationships between the leading capitalist centers and the ex-colonies, part of a complex web of economic and political connections referred to by some scholars as relations between the "core and periphery," based on the "dependency" of the poor countries upon the economic structure of capitalism as embodied in a "world system." As we look for the patterns of economic coercion that have replaced colonialism in the Americas, we might do well to start in the 19th century.

In the 1800s, when the United States was expanding its borders so quickly and incorporating huge sums of British capital into its railroads, its steel mills, and many other industrial endeavors, there were also opportunities for large-scale capital to influence the growth and development of other parts of the Hemisphere. There were opportunities to reorganize production on favorable terms and make money, generally in agriculture and mining. Foreign capital flowed throughout the Americas, whether invited or uninvited, legal or illegal, and overpowered any hopes for democratic self-sufficiency. Three countries, Cuba, Mexico, and Chile, are discussed here as examples of the process which took place almost everywhere.

CUBA

Until the late 18th century Cuba had been an exception to the sugar plantation economy imposed upon the Caribbean islands by European invest-ment. Only a minority of its population was African, some of them slaves and others living freely as smallholders and farm workers. The major agricultural pursuits were cattle raising and tobacco growing on small farms which sometimes had a few slaves, sometimes black and white wage laborers.

After Britain invaded Havana in 1762, the large island remained under Spanish political control, but quickly surrendered itself to British economic influence. By the end of the century the British had financed the spread of plantations over former cattle lands and filled them up with slaves for sugar production; consequently dried beef, which before had been exported by Cuba in large quantities, now had to be imported to feed the slaves. As the 19th century progressed, Great Britain and the United States had an unwritten agreement, backed up implicitly by the Monroe Doctrine, to leave Cuba in Spanish hands while developing it as an economic resource. Cuba began to displace the other islands as the primary sugar producer; and England, no longer in need of a slave trade, abolished it in 1808.

In the 19th century, 550,000 slaves were imported to Cuba. By 1894, Cuba produced 30% of the world's cane sugar.

Cuba had an advantage over the other Caribbean islands that was due to more than its superior size. Eric Williams, in his *History of the Caribbean: from Columbus to Castro*, explained why Cuba produced 1,458,342 tons of sugar in 1894 compared to only 404,128 tons for the rest of the Caribbean:

1. The soil was better, not having been exhausted already by the centuries of sugar monoculture. Many other islands were ecological disasters.

2. Cuban plantations were large corporate affairs using modern techniques; they replaced the 350 year old trapiche mill (driven by horses or oxen) with steam power; other islands still had 18th century operations.

3. Rail lines were used to link plantations to mills, then to connect the mills to refineries and sea transport.

Industrialization of agricultural production proceeded hand in hand with slave labor as long as the labor requirements could not be met with the available population. When slavery in Cuba was abolished and replaced by wage labor in 1880, there was a large impoverished population which could be set in competition for subsistence wages and laid off in the off-season. Cuba's huge share of world cane sugar production was remarkable, particularly since many other countries were being pressed into duty as highly efficient capitalist agro-exporters of sugar: Mexico, Hawaii, and the Philippines were a few of them.

At the end of the 19th century, some of the largest plantations in Cuba were owned by U.S. companies and Spanish rule was weaker than ever. After three years of local armed revolt inspired by Jose Marti had nearly brought about the collapse of colonial rule, the U.S. gave in to its overwhelming desire to acquire colonies and invaded the island. Theodore Roosevelt wrote to a friend a year before the Spanish American War began: "I should welcome almost any war, for I think this country needs one."

By 1901, U.S. companies controlled all the economic resources of the rich island; it was clear that the imperialist mission had been fulfilled. Henry Cabot Lodge, Senator from Massachusetts, had predicted this in the 1890s when he wrote:

> *"The island of Cuba.. will become a necessity... The great nations are rapidly absorbing for their future expansion all the waste nations of the earth. It is a movement which makes for civilization and the advancement of the race."*

With all this loot in hand, the U.S. refused to let Cubans exercise the freedom to rule themselves and instead kept Cuba as a kind of protectorate. Later, in the 1930s, a corrupt Cuban Army officer named Batista assumed dictatorial powers on terms that were very friendly to U.S. capital.

In 1958, a year before Fidel Castro's revolution successfully removed Batista from power, Cuba epitomized the highest degree of neo-colonial exploitation:

- U.S. sugar companies controlled 75% of Cuba's arable land.
- Sugar accounted for 90% of Cuba's exports, 33% of its national income.

Consequently the rural population lived in excruciating poverty:

- only 4% of the peasantry ate meat as a regular part of their diet; 1% ate fish, none ate fresh vegetables; 11% drank milk, and 2% ate eggs.
- 61% of the rural children did not attend school.

Contrary to the North American myth, Fidel Castro did not fool the Cuban population into accepting a socialist revolution. Whatever the limitations of his government, due both to unrelenting external economic pressure from the U.S. and the internal resistance to democratic institutions, it has served the poor (meaning 90% of the population) infinitely better than the old regime of the sugar barons, which provided a mafia-encrusted playground for the idle rich from the United States but no social welfare programs of any kind. Today Cuba's education and medical systems are the envy of all developing countries and its economy, though struggling, should not be compared to drug-fueled Miami, home of many affluent Cubans who fled revolutionary Cuba. Cuba should stand review in the company of the real human disaster stories of the Western Hemisphere - countries in Central America, South America, and the Caribbean which have tried to be good "capitalist models" of development since the 1950s, but have utterly disappointed the majority of their people in the process.

MEXICO

At the end of the 19th century large parts of Mexico had gone the way of Cuba, converting rapidly toward totally capitalistic development of agriculture. In Morelos, the state from which Emilio Zapata would lead the Mexican Revolution in 1911, 25% of the land was owned by just 17 people and sugar mills were sprouting up to service efficient sugar plantations which were considered - after Puerto Rico and Hawaii - to be the most productive in the world.

In 1910, the census of all of Mexico told an overwhelming story: Mexico was not some vast collection of "feudal" estates lost in another era; it was instead tied into a system of primitive capitalist agriculture:

- of all Mexican heads of family, 96.6% held no land at all.
- 80% of Mexico's population depended upon agricultural wages.

As the century began, "wage peonage" or "wage slavery" had tied down 12 million out of 15 million Mexicans, by legal contract or inherited debt, to the cultivation of various export crops: "on Yucatan henequen plantations, on the tobacco plantations of the Valle Nacional, on Chiapas and Tabasco timberland and fruit orchards, and on the rubber, coffee, sugarcane, tobacco and fruit plantations of Vera Cruz, Oaxaca, and Morelos."

With half of the cultivatible land in the hands of only 1.5% of the landlords, Mexico was also a favorite site for U.S. investment; of all U.S. capital invested abroad at the turn of the 20th century, one third was in Mexico. As John Kenneth Turner wrote in 1910, "The Americanization of Mexico of which Wall Street boasts is being accomplished with a vengeance."

Mexico had endured the era of the "Porfiriato," the reign of President Porfirio Diaz, who was determined to grant all kinds of concessions to North American investors in order to "modernize" Mexico. At the beginning of his rule in 1881, the

U.S. already received 42% of Mexico's mineral exports, but by the end, 1909, it controlled 77%. Guggenheim and other U.S. firms took over the mining industry and built railroads which ran from source to port all over Mexico; often they applied new mining techniques to the richest of the old mines, like Cerro de San Pedro in San Luis Potosí; there, the Americans extracted not only silver, but lead and gold, too.

With its small class of wealthy landowners and military opportunists cooperating with big capital from the North while the huge proportion of dispossessed rural poor looked on in bewilderment, Mexico was ripe for a Revolution. "Modernization" meant desperation for most people. Led by peasant soldiers like Zapata in the South, and bandit heroes like Pancho Villa in the North, the armies of the poor swept over the country with a vengeance. The outcome of the Revolution was mixed: Mexico made some efforts towards land reform while some empty anti-capitalist rhetoric still lives on within the dominant and corrupt PRI ("Institutionalized Revolutionary Party"); on the other hand, real economic power has remained under the control of a tiny elite of capitalists and U.S.-trained bureaucrats, a kind of "consular bourgeoisie" who can do the bidding of corporations and banks in the North.

In the 1980s, the profits of the transnational corporations were shipped out of Mexico to the advanced capitalist countries, and the capital surplus which elite Mexicans squeeze out of the rest of the population was quickly exported to North America for investment in real estate and other hedges against inflation. Thus Mexico was deprived of the primary means by which it could alleviate its massive indebtedness. In just five years in the 1980s the amount of money removed from Mexico by its privileged elite was equal to about 2/3 of the foreign debt: Mexican capital flight amounted to $63 billion.

CHILE

Perhaps the saddest story of neo-colonial manipulation has taken place in Chile, a country with a small population, vast resources and a reputation for trying to make democracy work. Here history repeated itself ingloriously, as two presidents who were intent on promoting economic self-sufficiency and the social welfare of the majority were eliminated by the capitalist forces which controlled the most valuable parts of the economy.

In the late 19th century, British investors were everywhere in the world purchasing influence. In 1884 they financed the "Nitrate War" for Chile,

whose soldiers wore British uniforms and carried British rifles. Chile defeated both Peru and Bolivia, which had previously laid claim to the Pacific desert areas north of Chile; these barren lands were home to the world's most valuable sources of nitrate, so very useful for making both fertilizers and explosives.

In 1886, a reformer named Balmaceda was elected President of Chile. In 1888 he unveiled a plan to nationalize the nitrate industries by buying out the British. The investment community in Britain provoked an uproar in the London press, where Balmaceda was called a "butcher" and a "dictator of the worst sort." Then the English promoted a fake "civil war" on the Peruvian border and decried the danger which the unstable Chilean government posed to their investments. British warships were called upon to blockade Chilean ports until Balmaceda was defeated. The President, despondent over his failure to institute progressive reforms and lacking any widespread political network to resist the British, committed suicide. By 1890, 3/4 of all Chilean exports went through Great Britain.

Not so much later, in 1915, the nitrate market collapsed entirely when the Germans perfected artificial manufacturing processes. By the 1920s U.S. investors had replaced the British as primary exploiters of Chile's minerals, this time the vast deposits of copper which were so essential to the rapidly growing electrical industry. As in Mexico the Guggenheim fortune was involved, from which the corporate entities of Anaconda and Kennecott Copper evolved. Between 1920 and 1970 Anaconda and Kennecott took more than $4 billion in profits out of Chile, many times over what they had invested. As of 1964 the average wage in a Chilean copper mine was only 1/8 of the Kennecott refinery wage in the U.S.

In 1970, after having run for President again and again for twenty years, Socialist candidate Salvador Allende was elected President of Chile. He promised to nationalize the copper mines, while compensating the U.S. companies only modestly since they had so thoroughly exploited Chile already. This threat led the the U.S. representative in Chile, Ambassador Korry, to articulate the U.S. counter-threat in a message he sent to Washington even before Allende took office:

> *"Not a nut or bolt shall reach Chile under Allende. Once Allende comes to power we shall do all within our power to condemn Chile and all Chileans to utmost deprivation and poverty."*

From 1970 to 1973, Allende instituted economic reforms in addition to the nationalizations, and ran an exemplary democratic government which was promoting a mixed economy. In the U.S. White House, Richard Nixon and his national security advisor, Henry Kissinger, fumed and fussed and set their CIA plan to work. Severe economic sanctions by the U.S. were accompanied by work stoppages and trucking strikes financed by the CIA. Economic conditions became tighter for some, including upper middle class housewifes who could not buy all the foreign goodies they were accustomed to enjoy; they were persuaded by right-wing political parties to bang their pots and pans in the streets.

In the meantime, despite the foreign harassment, Allende and his leftist allies gained in popularity, to the extent that they were gaining an absolute majority in the Chilean Congress. In the countryside and the cities, poor peasants and workers, more radical than the government, were finding ways to control the property owned by absentee owners. For instance, in the capital of Santiago, a group of about 400 workers simply took over the operation of a large food processing factory and disregarded the owners who lived in North America. They organized production on a collective basis, with equal hourly pay for all, and added a second shift so that production increased dramatically. Wages went up and so did the surplus earned from their efforts; some of the surplus, which formerly would have left the country as profits for the foreign owners, went to fund mobile soup kitchens - vans staffed by factory members cruised the poor neighborhoods of Santiago giving free meals, products made in their factory, to the hungry.

Economic pressure on Allende was not working and neither was media propaganda. Before his election in 1970 the CIA had implemented scare campaigns in certain Chilean newspapers which it secretly funded, in an attempt to portray Allende as a Communist menace. One doctored photo sequence showed Soviet tanks chugging around in front of La Moneda, the presidential palace - a CIA fantasy of what democratic socialism would bring to Chile. Ironically, it was Chile's own tanks that cruised up the avenues of Santiago in 1973 to fire upon Allende as the air force strafed and bombed the palace from above. Most of the Chilean Generals had been conspiring with the U.S. since 1970 to stage a military coup if and when it was necessary. After assassinating the Army chief of staff who was loyal to Allende, the Chilean generals, under the leadership of Augusto Pinochet and with offshore coordination provided by U.S. Navy ships, moved in for the kill. President Allende picked up a submachine gun and died fighting his own troops as they attacked the palace.

As has so often been the case throughout Latin America, the general who collaborated with the U.S. thereby earned the right to rule. Pinochet stood staunchly as the free-market dictator and President of Chile from 1973 to 1989, a time that marked the generalized use of terror and death squads throughout much of Latin America. Thousands of Pinochet's political enemies were "disappeared" in late 1973, and one million of Chile's ten million people had to flee to safety in other countries. The generals in Argentina and Uruguay noted the easy acceptance of state terror by the U.S. State Department and decided to follow Pinochet's example in their own countries. The copper mines were, of course, returned to U.S. companies and a whole crew of "Chicago boys," ultra-conservative economists trained at the University of Chicago, were brought in to reverse the democratic trends of the early seventies.

With state terror and economic austerity providing efficient discipline of the work force, the Chilean economy was able to improve its exports and earnings on foreign exchange (a favorable comparison with the Allende years was not so difficult to achieve since foreign loans and avenues of exchange for the Allende government had been shut down by the United States.) Although some of the Chicago economists say that the Pinochet years spelled success for the Chilean economy, reality was much bleaker: wages dropped sharply for 80% of Chilean workers while social services and medical systems were dismantled. Most people, in accordance with the five hundred year old American tradition, were being further exploited in the service of foreign trade.

Chapter 16

AMERICAN FREEDOM MEANS THE FREEDOM TO INVEST

After World War II, when the United States was uncontestedly the world's richest nation, it treasured no freedom more than the freedom to invest around the world. Third World investments were particularly profitable:

1950-1965

New U.S. Investment Going to the Third World: $9.0 billion

Profits from the Third World Returning to U.S.: $25.6 billion

By the 1970s the world economy was stagnant. The banks of the United States and other advanced capitalist nations sought high profits by making ill-conceived loans to countries in the Third World:

The Percentage of Profits Coming from International Loans
(for the 12 Largest U.S. Banks)

1970 - 17%   **1977** - 49%

By the 1980s Latin America and other poor regions of the world were incapacitated by the extraordinary debts and high interest rates owed to the banking countries:

1987	Brazilian Foreign Debt	Mexican Foreign Debt
	$124 Billion	$107 billion

AMERICAN FREEDOM MEANS THE FREEDOM TO INVEST

In the 1980s much of the Third World suffered an absolute worsening of its economic condition, as depression conditions and an extreme state of indebtedness combined to lower the standard of living of most people. The success in manufacturing and world trade achieved by a few small industrializing countries, like South Korea and Taiwan for example, did little to offset the disadvantages besetting the over 4 billion people who live outside the advanced capitalist nations. (These high income countries, as defined by the World Bank, include the original European core; their offshoots: the United States, Canada, Australia and New Zealand; Japan; and a few small oil producers.)

In the last two decades most of the Latin American debt was secured from U.S. banks at very high interest rates, the highest rates since the Great Depression of the 1930s. Two of the largest countries in America, Brazil and Mexico, which together have more land area than the United States and almost as many people, were being crushed by the overwhelming debt incurred by corrupt governments and businessmen in collusion with overly greedy bankers in the North.

Brazil and Mexico not only endured a debt crisis, but they began the process of an industrial revolution that promises to be more brutal than anything the advanced capitalist countries ever had to endure. Their people, who have suffered drastic cutbacks in their already meager standards of living on behalf of "modernization," have been looking for a way to avoid this kind of capitalist development. In recent elections in both countries, parties of the left nearly defeated the U.S.-backed candidates by advocating a fairer distribution of wealth and the possible repudiation of their foreign debt.

In Mexico, there was so much election fraud in 1988 that many observers are quite certain that Cuauhtemoc Cardenas, the leader of the left coalition, had the election stolen from him. The winner, candidate of the thoroughly corrupted Institutionalized Revolutionary Party, Carlos Salinas, is a Harvard-trained economist and former finance minister who was more than willing to cut back further on social services in order to faithfully service the debt to the U.S. and the International Monetary Fund. Cardenas, in contrast, is the son of the one truly popular President who ruled Mexico during this century, Lazaro Cardenas. During his years of rule, the elder Cardenas instituted genuine reforms, redistributed land to the peasants and increased the well-being of the working class. In 1938

he defied Britain and the U.S. and nationalized their oil companies. Perhaps it was purposeful that he named his son Cuauhtemoc, the name of the King Montezuma's son, the valiant Aztec warrior who raised an army in an attempt to drive out the Spanish conquistadors. Now the modern day Cuauhtemoc faces the equally formidable task of fighting off the U.S. imperialists.

In Brazil, the imagery of war, of punishment hidden in the garb of paternalistic "development," is central to Luis da Silva's explication of the suffering that afflicts his country and all the other victims of the global system:

"I will tell you that the Third World War has already started - a silent war, not for that reason any less sinister. This war is tearing down Brazil, Latin America, and practically all the Third World. Instead of soldiers dying, there are children dying; instead of millions of wounded, there are millions of unemployed; instead of the destruction of bridges, there is the tearing down of factories, schools, hospitals, and entire communities."

Da Silva, who leads the Metal Workers' Union, nearly won the 1989 presidential election with 45% of the vote for his socialist Workers' Party. "Lula," as he is known, and his party have a vast grassroots organization of poor people which depends on the close cooperation of many thousands of Christian base communities. The Workers Party nearly overcame the severe disadvantages of unequal media access to defeat the Establishment candidate, Fernando Collor.

Collor, from a wealthy family, used his access to a TV and publishing empire to make false promises to the millions of homeless people and squatters who flock to the Brazilian cities. In reality, he was planning to institute the harshest of economic shocks immediately upon taking office. The severe recession that he induced with these measures was applauded in the United States as "realistic," and immediately the International Monetary Fund agreed to grant new loans because it approved of the imposition of austerity. Alexander Cockburn has termed Collor's shock treatment "the newly emerging world model" of "market discipline."

The Bush Administration in Washington called Collor "bold" and did not object when the new President indicated that government repression might accompany induced recession. After a major opposition newspaper printed a picture of him in military uniform over the caption, "Third World Mussolini," he sent armed police into the newspaper's offices to take prisoners. This immediately reminded Brazilians of their recent past.

From 1964 to 1986 Brazil had been ruled by another "austerity government" after the CIA had encouraged Brazilian generals to depose the left-leaning elected government of President Goulart. Their first order of business in 1964 was to clamp a freeze on workers' wages and begin adding to a tiny foreign debt of $2 million. By 1984, shortly before they gave up power to a partly civilian government, the generals had accumulated a debt of $100 billion. Brazil had grown to be the world's eighth largest economy during that time, but unprecedented poverty and ecological damage had arrived at the same time. "Public spending on health, education, housing and nutrition had declined steadily since the military coup," according to the North American Committee on Latin America. Workers' wages had declined by 40%.

Brazil's efforts to industrialize over the last thirty years had considerable success because the military junta and their business allies were so willing to impose hardships upon 80% of the people. Today 2/3 of Brazil's exports are industrial, a very rare achievement in a part of the world where exports have generally been agricultural or mineral. But recently the industries owned by Brazilian nationals and by the State have been failing, partly due to their overwhelming debt; meanwhile, multinational companies loaded with cash, like Volkswagon, have been taking the lead in auto production by investing in new plants in new areas. They are choosing parts of the country where labor is cheap and non-militant, just like Japanese companies operating in the United States (Nissan chose to locate its big North American plant in a poor part of Tennessee so it could employ non-union labor at lower wages.)

Mexico, perhaps because of its proximity to the United States, is further along than Brazil in its accommodation of foreign interests. A whole string of cities and factories now sits along the southern side of the Rio Grande eager to provide low wage assembly operations for U.S. multinational corporations. In 1987 Mexican workers were earning about $4 per day in General Motors plants compared to $16 per hour in Detroit. GM had 17 plants in Mexico and was building 12 more to replace factories slated for closing in the United States. When General Motors built a plant in Ramos Arizpe near the U.S. border, an important geographical consideration was not only the proximity to the U.S. but also the distance from Mexico City, where the strong labor union movement could exert its influence. Consequently GM was able to pay its Mexican workers only 50–60% of the Mexico City wage and make them work 7 or 8 hours longer each week.

The U.S. auto industry is becoming thoroughly internationalized, with the emphasis being on locating cheap and docile labor. By 1990 there were approximately 300,000 autos imported from Mexico, a figure which underscored the big change in auto trade:

Auto Trade: U.S. - Latin America

	1981	1986
U.S. Auto Exports to Latin America	$3.6 billion	$2.7 billion
U.S. Auto Imports from Latin America	$0.8 billion	$4.2 billion
Auto Trade Balance	+$2.8 billion	-$1.5 billion

This kind of international industrial manipulation, based on the best conditions for exploiting labor, has become an important factor in undermining the strength of unions and the wages of working class people in the United States. Since 1973, weekly earnings in the U.S. have declined by about 19%, even though the gross domestic product per capita was rising. The U.S. worker, who had enjoyed about 40 years of great prosperity compared to his counterparts in the rest of America, was becoming "Latin Americanized"; that is, U.S. society was becoming further divided between rich and poor as U.S.capitalists and bankers increasingly looked to the world labor market, and authoritarian discipline of labor forces, as the solution to producing high profits on their investments.

Capitalism, just as it was celebrating the fall of the twisted version of socialism that had oppressed Eastern Europe, was falling back on the time-honored method of extracting profit: coercing labor. There used to be a classic notion, common to Marxism as well as to liberal economic thought, that capitalist expansion of industry would bring positive capitalist development to the poor countries of the world. Scholars Volker Bornschier and Christopher Chase Dunn challenged this idea in their book, *Transnational Corporations and Underdevelopment*. They predicted the trend that is being seen all over the world:

> Countries with growing foreign investment by transnational corporations (or TNCs) "will experience economic stagnation, under- and un- employment, and increased marginalization... relative to countries which are less penetrated by TNCs."

In most cases, the kind of capitalist development directed by transnational companies in the Third World will benefit from conditions which create or maintain an oversupply of cheap and hungry labor. The wage laborers in the South can be used up and tossed aside as the profits travel northward, in much the same way as slaves and virgin land were exploited to the maximum and then abandoned two or three centuries ago.

71

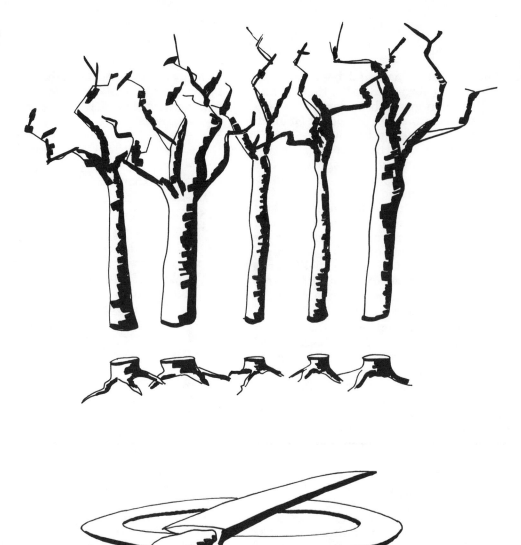

Chapter 17

EXPLOITING THE LAST FRONTIER: THE AMAZON RAINFOREST

The willingness of Europeans and other capitalists to dispose of nature, to use it up and throw it away, has often been foreshadowed by their willingness to dispose of other human beings.

1495 - Columbus ordered each male Indian on Hispaniola to deliver a flask of gold every three months. Those who failed had their hands chopped off.

1903 - In the Congo, the Belgian traders were chopping off the hands of Africans who could not deliver enough wild rubber. The population of the Congo decreased by 50%.

1912 - The Peruvian Amazon Company, capitalized on the London stock market, enslaved Amazonian Indians in the rainforest for the purpose of collecting rubber. Here, too, chopping off hands was a favorite form of labor discipline. The native population suddenly declined by 80%.

1988 - Chico Mendes, head of the Brazilian Rubber Tappers Union and a grassroots ecologist, was assassinated by cattle ranchers for his efforts to preserve the rainforest and the people who live in it.

"In the Amazon, when trees fall people die." - Susanna Hecht

EXPLOITING THE LAST FRONTIER: THE AMAZON RAINFOREST

Chico Mendes was proposing the establishment of "protective reserves" in the Brazilian rainforest, large areas which would be protected from the devastation of mining and cattle raising. These reserves could sustain economic activities, limited ones like collecting rubber and nuts, which do not threaten the existence of the forest. Mendes died because the world lives by a different logic, the system of maximum profitability that yearns to exploit every possible resource.

Presently the whole earth is governed to some extent by the rules of a capitalist world system, but this is hardly a smoothly working "capitalist empire" imposing a strict order on all economic and ecological activity. At the end of the 20th century, a flurry of capitalist disorder seems to reign, when profit-making impulses and investments at various levels, sometimes coordinated and other times at odds, are tearing into the last untouched fabric of the earth. Thus, when we look at the Amazon rainforest, we cannot look for single causes on which to vent our anger. Some leftist critics have laid the blame on transnational corporations which conspire to sell hamburgers; their instincts may be correct, but they do not adequately understand the problem. On the other hand, there is the neo-Malthusian enthusiasm of rich Northerners who agonize over Third World population increases while they are consuming the bulk of the world's resources. Their elitist point of view becomes a way of deflecting the blame away from the capitalist centers of power.

In the interest of giving some explanation to the plight of the rainforest in South America, let us review some of the factors which simultaneously contribute to the assault on the Amazon:

1. Generalized Profitability: Brazil, like many parts of the world that have been pushed suddenly toward further integration into the world capitalist system, has lived under repressive neo-fascist regimes (a military junta ruled Brazil from 1964 to 1985). The major thrust of such regimes is to encourage the profitable exploitation of labor and natural resources. The Amazon represents resources to be used, but not just by one group.

2. Exploitative Agriculture, large scale: the government has sold huge tracts of land to wealthy developers and corporations at very low prices. 23 of 28 of the largest landowners in Brazil are owners of parcels in Amazonia; their holdings total 60 million acres. In the state of Acre at the upper end of the Amazon, 33 million acres were sold to big developers between 1971 and 1975; at the beginning of that short period the state was 75% publicly owned or unclaimed, afterwards it was 80% privately owned. According to Susanna Hecht and Alexander Cockburn in their book, *The Fate of the Forest*, these large holdings were the ones that were eligible for government loans, grants, subsidies, and tax credits. These fiscal incentives were the only thing that made raising cattle - the primary activity on these huge holdings - into an even marginally profitable activity. Actually, this beef production does not provide many hamburgers for McDonalds, but instead goes mostly to domestic food production. The best Brazilian land is already being used for export agriculture - coffee, oranges, soybeans, sugar, cocoa, etc. - hence two thirds of Brazilians do not get enough to eat even though Brazil is one of the wealthiest countries in the Third World.

3. Exploitative Agriculture, small scale: the expansion of large scale export agriculture (70% of the land is owned by fewer than 4% of the farm owners) has pushed 25 million Brazilians off their lands in the past two decades; most of these people become a vast pool of low-cost wage labor in the cities, but many of them head for the frontier areas of the forest, where they burn down the trees and to try to eke out a living on small farm plots. Since the soil is inherently weak in most areas, it is exhausted for crop raising in 2 to 5 years. Some small landowners then acquire a few cattle and expand their holdings; others sell the land cheaply to large cattle ranchers and move further into the rain forest to create new farms by destroying more trees.

4. Exploitative Mining, small scale: refugee adventurers, displaced from their old farms or fleeing the city favelas, or slums, go looking for gold in the alluvial deposits throughout the Amazon basin, especially in the untouched areas predominately inhabited by Indians. Miners, with the help of soldiers and cattle ranchers, have reason to remove (meaning kill) the Indians who claim the area as their hunting and gathering ground.

5. Exploitative Corporate Mining: because Brazil is trying so hard to industrialize, it wants to use its own iron resources in the Amazon. After large scale industrial mining destroys parts of the forest, hundreds of thousands of square miles of trees are cut down to produce charcoal, the cheapest fuel for the smelters because Brazil has no coal deposits.

6. The Pressure of Debt: during the rule of the military, the generals allied themselves with the wealthy business class which was eager to enlarge its fortunes in both agriculture and industry; the government borrowed heavily from international banks in both the U.S.and the other advanced industrial countries. Now, with a foreign debt of over $100 billion, there is a reluctance to curtail any of the exploitative mining and agriculture which might produce some foreign exchange.

7. Pressure from Banks of the North: the First World solution to extravagant debt is to require more exploitation of people; or, if one prefers the rationale of the International Monetary Fund, more "austerity" is necessary to permit the Brazilian people to meet their "obligations," that is, to pay the debt incurred by past dictatorships. Workers' incomes declined by 40% in the 1980s and export industries have been emphasized even more than before; producing for the basic needs of Brazilian families is considered wasteful.

THE ECOLOGICAL NIGHTMARE

Brazil has followed the New World capitalist path since the 16th century: land was first developed with Indian and African slaves for export agriculture and mineral extraction, consequently it has always been monopolized by a few people. The first product of the rainforest to be ruthlessly used up and thrown away was the Indian population, which was rounded up for sale to the plantations and mines. As the agro-export industries were modernized and expanded in the 19th and 20th centuries, more and more people were displaced from the land and freed up for subsistence wage labor in both agriculture and the new, developing industries in manufacturing. Mining and timber operations in the Amazon basin usually produce badly needed foreign exchange, so are encouraged despite the tremendous environmental damage they inflict.

Such is the progress of civilization. One of the leaders of the Brazilian junta proclaimed that their government's purpose was

"to inundate the Amazon forest with civilization."

Unlimited expansion is the very life blood of capitalism; and capitalists, whether those in Brazil who are "inundating" the Amazon or those in the United States, Europe, or Japan who are funding the process or setting up their own transnational factories, have no idea of how to limit the effects of their rapacity. Since the beginning of the European invasion, America has been a place to be deflowered by virile entrepreneurs:

"A country that hath yet her maidenhead, never sacked, turned, nor wrought."

- Sir Walter Raleigh, writing to Queen Elizabeth of England in 1600 to tell her of the desirable virgin land in Guiana on the northeast coast of South America.

Now that the advanced industrial countries of the North are beginning to worry about the global implications of exploiting nature, they have panicked about the significance of the Amazon for their own survival. What if the burning of the rainforest contributes too much to global warming? What if the multitudinous animal species of the jungle are lost forever? What if too many rich Brazilians, and their elite counterparts throughout the Third World, drive their air-conditioned cars down new jungle highways and help destroy the ozone layer with the carbons and chlorofluorocarbons they produce?

The Amazon, the symbol of lost innocence, is certainly crucial to the earth's survival. Even more important, however, is the need for the Northerners to review their own way of life, the corporate commodity culture that has spread everywhere, even to the rain forest. No matter how many pollutants the producers and consumers in the Third World pour into the atmosphere, they will have a difficult time equalling the pollution created by the earth's minority of rich people in the North, who are also the ones collecting the bulk of the high interest payments and profits created by the pollution in the South.

The people of the North ought to feel obligated to somehow contribute their monetary resources to maintaining the natural resources of the South. For the Brazilian people, the solution is to say "no" to the economic forces that have controlled their destiny. Twenty-five years of erstwhile industrial development, zealously copying the capitalist powers, impoverished over 100 million people. In 1990, local and international capitalists could only offer more of the same: an austerity government futilely tightening the screws on behalf of the "free market."

The remedy, or a path toward finding the remedy, was offered by the Workers' Party in the 1989 election. This party is an unusual kind of socialist party for Latin America because it has been organized primarily from the grassroots upwards, by the very people who have been exploited rather than by a sympathetic group of intellectuals in the upper classes. Luis da Silva, the Presidential candidate and a member of Congress, is very representative of the people, a metal worker by trade who has a sixth grade education. And the mayor of Sao Paulo, Luiza Erundina, is a refugee from Brazil's poorest area, the sugar-growing state of Bahia; she worked for years as a low-paid social worker.

The Workers' Party wants to stem the flow of capital out of Brazil; they feel that the $12 billion a year that services the foreign debt should be used inside Brazil. A similar amount of money is transported out of the troubled economy through "capital flight," as the profits and assets of the Brazilian elite are being exported toward investments in other parts of the world. The Workers' Party suggests that some of this money should be used to alleviate the terrible social conditions that afflict the Brazilian majority; the greater share would go toward creating economic democracy, that is, shares in the ownership of Brazilian in-dustry would be purchased by the workers' themselves.

The most important reform addresses the "original sin" of the European conquest of Brazil and the rest of America, the monopolization of land for export crops. Not only must land be retained for the Indians and the rubber tappers, but the vast holdings of the "fazendeiros," the big landowners, need to be redistributed to the landless peasants. Studies have shown that Brazil's small farms are much more productive than the large ones; those under 250 acres cover only 1/5 of Brazil's arable land but produce most of the food eaten in Brazil. Land redistribution would immediately give Brazil the capacity of feeding all its people adequately; it would also end the grievous inequality of wealth that now forces millions of peasants to seek survival by invading the rainforest.

Part IV

NORTH VERSUS SOUTH

The patterns of development in the American Hemisphere have been incredibly unequal, granting growth and riches to the North at the expense of the misery and exploitation of the South. The patterns in America also served as the general guidelines for capitalist development around the world. Even though the program of genocide was not usually as complete outside of the Western Hemisphere, white men from the North still succeeded in subduing the other parts of the globe.

In Africa and Asia - which are also lumped together under the descriptive term, "South," to designate those on the "bottom" of the globe and the world social system - the super-exploitation of human labor was also benefiting the centers of European capital. Slavery or indentured work on plantations and forced labor in mineral production were common features of colonization around the globe, whether in British South Africa, French West Africa, British India, German Southwest Africa, French Indochina, or Dutch Indonesia. The very recent independence movements in these parts of the globe, which took advantage of the weak state of the capitalist countries after they tried to destroy each other in World War II, did not really sever the old links to the world capitalist system. The era of national liberation movements around the world, from about 1945 to 1975, has passed. Since then, the chances for these countries to pursue a course of development outside of capitalism have quickly faded.

Now, with the ending of the Cold War, the fading of East-West distinctions makes the North-South dichotomy look clearer than ever. Thus it is imperative that we spend some time reflecting on the state of the whole world, on the nature of a truly internationalized capitalist system which cannot be easily reformed or redirected in one part of the world at a time. We must keep in mind that the relentless drive for profit and the corresponding flood of commodity mania that characterizes capitalism is not aimless madness, even though these attributes may render the system blind and unresponsive to even the gravest calamities, such as the ecological destruction of the globe. Capitalism has a narrowly focused dynamism, whether mad or not, which is capable of nimble movements in search of ever more productive methods and sites around the world. The wealth it has produced is now capable of sustaining adequate standards of living for the entire population of the globe, yet the system is utterly incapable of arranging for the few to share with the many.

Even as the North keeps growing richer at the expense of the South, the situation is anything but static. The U.S. is going through economic turmoil and losing its leading role in world manufacturing and financial affairs, while other countries are emerging as new players in squeezing out the maximum profits, or surplus value, from their own working classes. Defenders of capitalism will point to this change and dynamism and tell us to look to the good side of things in the emerging capitalist nations like Taiwan and South Korea, or the frantic little city states like Singapore and Hong Kong.

In the next chapter, we will briefly examine South Korea, home of economic miracles and political repression, because it is so often held up as the model of economic development other countries must emulate. In the following chapters we will try to catch a glimpse of some the ways which the industrialized North, led by the military might of the United States, still manages to impose its economic and political will upon most parts of the earth. This new kind of imperialism, although distinct from old colonialism, can still force the Third World to serve as a "plantation" for the white (and Japanese) centers of capital. Industrial plantations are now cultivatable in a great many places. That is, a huge number of unemployed or underemployed workers are gathered in the big and small cities of the Third World and disciplined by hunger, desperation, international competition, and local police states in such a way that they can now produce a great many of the world's industrial goods at a tiny fraction of the cost of the wages of workers in the capitalist core. Although idle land, emptied of its former inhabitants, lies available for traditional plantations, the more important development resources today are the cities and shanty towns which overflow with people, the unused labor power which is so cheap that it seems almost as "free" as the land the conquistadors seized five hundred years ago.

Is this the next step in "post-industrialism", whereby the wealthy countries, 10% to 15% of the world's population, simply transport their industrial plants to the Third World? Can the world's environment survive this onslaught of industrialization? Will the exploited countries be able to take over control of their own productive powers? Or will the core group of advanced Northern countries persist in pushing them, and themselves, further towards a new era of barbarism?

Chapter 18

SOUTH KOREA - THE DEVELOPMENT MODEL

May 1980 - The Kwangju Massacre: 2,000 people were killed by the Korean Army when it attacked the civilian population of the city of Kwangju.

It became a criminal offense to discuss Kwangju.

1987-1990 As military rule gave way to partial democratization under former General Roh Tae Woo, thousands of new labor unions were formed. There were over 7,000 strikes.

May 1990 - 13,500 riot police invaded the giant Hyundai shipyards in Ulsan to try to put an end to a strike in the world's largest shipbuilding factory.

2,000 police stormed the headquarters of the Korean Broadcasting System to arrest 400 striking network employees.

Why, if South Korea is such an economic success, are the Korean people rebelling against the system?

SOUTH KOREA-
THE DEVELOPMENT MODEL

Nine years before the Chinese democracy movement in Tiananmen Square, people throughout South Korea were demonstrating for freedom from their authoritarian military regime. When the secret police began kidnapping and killing demonstrators in Kwangju, there was a democratic uprising by the citizens, who controlled their city for a week. Then the rebellion was crushed by Army divisions invading the city. But the Korean people never gave up.

Labor unrest and political strife are part of the price South Korea is paying for being the capitalist "success story" of the late 20th century. South Korea's remarkable economic growth has seemed to negate the kinds of dependency theory that predicted continued domination of developing countries by the traditional centers of capitalist power. There seems to be room within the capitalist world system for a few countries, like South Korea and Taiwan, to leave their "developing" status behind and begin to operate within the framework of nations that are "developed;" already they have strong centers of indigenously owned capitalist production and the technical expertise to set up their own export platforms in poorer countries.

The price of admission into the ranks of the developed countries appears to be very high: sustained government repression of democratic activity was necessary to create conditions in which labor could be exploited regularly and profitably. The process of subjugating Korean workers began many years ago in 1910, when Japan invaded Korea. The Japanese eradicated many vestiges of older, semi-feudalistic Korean culture and turned the country into a virtual prison labor camp which produced food and raw materials to fuel Japan's growing industrial plants and imperialistic war machine. In 1945, after the Japanese defeat in World War II, South Korea fell into the hands of the United States and has been occupied by U.S. troops ever since.

After the Korean War, the extreme anti-Communist political culture that was encouraged by the United States not only repressed political dissent, but also proved an invaluable rationale for enforcing and maintaining labor discipline over the working class. By the early 1980s total hourly compensation for Korean manufacturing workers (wages and benefits per hour) was only $1.22 per hour compared to $11.79 in the United States. One reason the production of manufactured goods could increase so quickly in South Korea was the complete disregard for workers' safety: it had the highest rate of industrial accidents and deaths in the world; 2.26% of its workers sustained serious injuries or died in the workplace every year, according to the International Labor Organization.

One important difference between South Korea and the developing countries of the American Hemisphere was the degree to which 20th century history and conflict wiped out the old culture and structural forms, thus creating a blank page for capitalist development. Another particular advantage in the early years of Korean development seems to have been the imposition of land reform, very popular with Koreans themselves and also backed by the American occupying forces. The redistribution of land to small independent farmers was one unequivocally positive result of U.S. intervention after World War II; it contributed to the successful industrial development of three Asian countries - Japan and Taiwan as well as South Korea. Land reform removed a certain amount of popular discontent by eliminating large scale inequality in the countryside and providing independent means of survival to some family units during the early years of industrialization. It also turned the eyes of local fledgling capitalists away from any ideas of agro-export business built on the subjection of the rural populations and instead concentrated their vision on industrial adaptations.

In the forty-five years since the end of World War II, Korea, like other developing countries, has undergone a massive change from a rural culture to an urban one through the mass migration of people to the cities. The teeming urban populations, like those in other parts of the world, have performed their customary role of providing an overabundance of low wage labor to new industries, Korean ones as well as U.S. and Japanese companies that came looking for cheap labor to assemble their electronic goods, shoes, etc. The cheapest labor, and often the most reliable, has been the labor of women. Women's docile performance under the watchful eye of local dictatorships convinced transnational corporations like RCA to stop television production in the U.S. and move it to Asia. Thorton Bradshaw, former chairman of RCA, once revealed the thoughts of U.S. corporate leaders about the special exploitation of Asian "girls:" their situation, he said, was an example of "the global village" at work; "the girls of Taiwan" deserved their chance to compete with the "girls of Indiana" because they wanted to join in the global consumer culture; as he so succinctly put it:

"The girls of Taiwan want their Mickey Mouse T-shirts, too."

Today women are initiating many of the widespread unionizing struggles that are underway in South Korea. Like women in most countries, they must wage a brave fight against the violence of male domination as well as against the forces of class domination. The massive wave of more than 7000 strikes in 1987–1990 was not met passively by the Korean corporations, which have long employed "Kusadae," or "Save-the-company-corps." The Kusadae are gangs of thugs who invade and patrol factories, beating up and otherwise intimidating workers in an attempt to drive out incipient unions. Foreign corporations generally have not employed the Kusadae, perhaps because they benefit indirectly from the anti-labor terror and need only pay wages that are slightly higher than the Korean companies. However, as the recent labor struggles have reached epic proportions, some American and Japanese companies have been taking advantage of the Kusadae squads; one subsidiary of the Tandy Corporation (Radio Shack products) called in the bullies to subdue its female workforce in 1988. They assisted the male managers of the plant in a brutal assault on women union leaders; several women were hung upside down, beaten, and sexually molested; 23 other new union members were sequestered and severely beaten until they signed resignation letters. The police were called to the scene but refused to interfere with internal company discipline.

The government tolerance of such oppressive behavior is built upon very close relationships between the State and business interests. These kinds of ties, which are often articulated in corporate/government linkages in the United States and developed to a higher level in the Japanese political economy, have reached a "high point" in Korea, where an exceptional degree of collusion exists between military rulers and the dominant giant business groups. The man elected President in 1988, Roh Tae Woo, was chosen to run for the office because of his loyalty to the Army: he was the General who rose quickly to the defense of General Chun when the latter assumed dictatorial power in the military coup of 1979. Roh's difficult job was to prove to the U.S. media that there is truly some "democracy" being practiced in Korea, while also guaranteeing his corporate allies that he can maintain or impose the "labor peace" by whatever means necessary.

The tight military-business oligarchy has been built around sufficient corruption - payments in cash and stock and property which satisfy the generals and other ranking officials - and a highly subsidized, extremely centralized core of giant Korean corporations, called "chaebol." The chaebol have been willing to fund the high costs of Korean election campaigns in recent years, which give an aura of legitimacy to an oppressive regime. The comment of one Korean senior executive at a medium-sized business group sums up the process:

"to put it in the simplest terms, who else is going to pay for all these elections?"

The concentration of wealth in Korean corporations is even more extreme than the high level of corporate control exhibited in the U.S.:

Concentration of Economic Power

1984 - The 100 largest U.S. corporations owned 61% of American business.

1983 - The 10 largest Korean corporations generated 64% of Korean GNP.

1989 - The 4 largest "chaebol" - Samsung, Hyundai, Daewoo, and Lucky-Goldstar - sold $105 billion in products, which was equal to 50% of the country's GNP.

Could the Korean example be a sign of further corporate "progress" in a recently developing country? The giant "chaebol" are now capable of competing on the world level with the biggest industrial countries. Japan has just commenced immense investment in the world's most sophisticated steel mills, nearly totally automated, in order to produce steel which can compete with its new Korean rivals. For the United States, interaction with the Korean giants is quite different, more like surrender. Not only is a chaebol like Hyundai, the world's biggest ship producer, marketing its cars successfully in America, but another company, Daewoo, is actually taking over production for General Motors. In a sparkling new production facility with technological features of a kind which GM is not often duplicating in its own American plants, Daewoo is producing the most sophisticated new cars in the Pontiac division and simply selling them to GM. Daewoo workers get paid better than most other Korean industrial laborers, but the cost is still many times less than it would be in U.S. auto plants.

SOUTH KOREA: A MODEL OR A WARNING?

Some economic conservatives would identify Korea as a model for Third World development, based on a culture of hard-working people combined with corporations and capitalists who are intent upon reinvesting in more production facilities. But they would have to admit that Korean success was achieved with a very unique set of supports from the United States: a constant military occupation and a stream of foreign aid; very favorable trade agreements which gave Korean companies great advantages in the U.S. market; heavy investment by U.S. corporations themselves in Korean export plants: and a remarkable tolerance by the U.S. for Korea's systematic repression of dissenting politicians and labor movements. By 1990, as Korea flexed its economic muscle, the United States withdrew some of the special trade and monetary privileges, which in turn created some economic difficulties for the Korean economy. Thus Korea's successful march into the upper capitalist ranks is by no means guaranteed.

Since Korean economic difficulties are occurring simultaneously with a great democratic upsurge from below, it will be difficult for the Roh Tae Woo regime to restore profitability by cutting back on wages, unless he eliminates the democratic movement. By March of 1990 he had pulled two opposition political parties into his coalition and was promising the business community that "labor peace" would be restored.

Korean workers, who during the period from 1965 to 1980 saw their standard of living rise, were very cognizant of the fact that the wealthy had gained far more during the same period; that is, the disparity between working people's income and upper class income was growing constantly greater. Korean political scientist Hang Yul Rhee states that most Koreans resent the fact that great wealth is being channeled to a very few people through the chaebol. Koreans, he says, are much more egalitarian-minded than North Americans, and will not accept the kinds of extreme of income distribution that prevail in the United States. U.S.-style inequality, he says, is a prescription for political havoc in Korea.

The example of Korea, which is relatively prosperous compared to other developing countries, seems to prove two things:

1. Industrial development which promotes internal economic growth is more difficult than it was 100 or 200 years ago because of the intense level of international competition.

2. Consequently, the conditions for achieving development require even harsher labor discipline and more sustained political repression than that which was imposed in the original capitalist countries when they began the industrial revolutions of the 18th and 19th centuries. In short, some form of fascism is required.

RELIGIOUS JUSTIFICATION

"Basically trying to take over the other person's mind. That's what the Third World War is all about. The war of ideology."

- Bo Hi Pak, Rev. Moon's top aid, former Korean military attache in the U.S., Chairman of CAUSA International.

In the battle of Korean capital to coerce the laboring population, the struggle for the laborers' minds has become ever more fervent. The development of a new cultural hegemony is key to the government's ability to maintain order, and, just as in several other parts of the world, this is a job to be undertaken by religious fundamentalists. Korea has had the largest growth of Christianity in Asia and, in recent years, the fastest growing fundamentalist evangelical movement anywhere in the world. Probably more than 30% of Korea is now Christian (with more than 2/3 of them being Protestant.). The Christian territory is contested, very much as in Latin America, between progressive forces allied to the Catholic Church and some old line Protestant denominations, and a rising conservative evangelical and neo-Pentecostal movement. Thus the Catholic Cardinal Kim and the Korean National Council of Churches (part of the World Council of Churches) have been supportive of the democracy movement and the labor uprisings; there is even a Korean variant on liberation theology, the religious option for the poor called "minjung."

As in Latin America, the conservative response has come from Pentecostal and neo-Pentecostal churches which have developed to serve the mass of displaced people of various classes who have thronged to the cities. One of the new churches claims what is by far the largest congregation in the world - the Full Gospel Central Church in Seoul has over 500,000 members. It's success at winning souls has been replicated in hundreds of smaller independent churches which excel in their entrepreneurial activity:

"It seems that the ancient practice known as 'sheep stealing' keeps the Christian pastors keen, lean - and efficient. Theirs is literally a spiritual enterprise culture."

The most remarkable, and most frightening, of Korean churches is the Unification Church of Reverend Sun Myung Moon, the extremely anti-Communist organization which has a worldwide network of "Moonies" who involve themselves in political interests and intrigues. Reverend Moon is a former Presbyterian minister who felt the call to start his own church, the Holy Spirit Association for the Unification of World Christianity. His theology, which one might think would be upsetting to many conservative Christians, features:

"a Korean messiah who supplants Jesus Christ and unifies the world under a single religious and political leader."

However, conservative anti-communist Christians, many of them in the United States, generally have no problem working closely with Reverend Moon. Although the "Moonies" do not have a large membership, they have cultivated invaluable ties; for instance, U.S. Congressional Committees exposed ties between the KCIA, the Korean Central Intelligence Agency, and a U.S. bank controlled by the Unification Church in 1978. Since then, the Church has become the owner of Washington D.C.'s second largest daily newspaper, *The Washington Times*, which publishes an unrelenting and influential New Right and Religious Right agenda. *The Times* led the support for such ventures as the Nicaraguan Freedom Fund, established in 1985 immediately after Congress denied funding to the Contras; the Fund sent $14 million in private money to keep the war going in Nicaragua.

The primary message of Moon, it seems, is in congruence with that of Pat Robertson and the other purveyors of Fundamentalist Americanism. He believes that communism and any kind of socialism are the work of Satan and that the United States and South Korea are God's vehicles for saving the world. Reverend Moon's mission, in his own words, is to establish a worldwide theocracy:

"to purge the corrupted politicians" so that *"the sons of God may rule the world."*

The cultural side of conquest is never so simple as the military/economic side, but there must emerge new methods of conquering the hearts and minds of those who must suffer through the next era of capitalist development. Long ago Spain's fear-inspiring brand of Catholicism helped overwhelm the original American cultures. Today another rigid brand of Christianity, fundamentalist Americanism, is spreading to various parts of the world at a rapid rate. In comparison with the clear political-economic endeavors of the North to control the South, the signs that cultural-religious systems are being created to smooth the way for global economic integration may look very vague and limited. At this point, we cannot claim that Protestant fundamentalism is destined to overpower all parts of the globe. What is apparent, however, is the need for a cultural adjustment, a coherent belief system, which helps the conquered

accept their new status as part of the working class in the world industrial and agricultural system.

In South Korea and Guatemala we can find new religious-ideological creations which serve the imperialist interests of the North, and the U.S. in particular. It would be comforting to think that these are temporary and localized eruptions which, although neo-fascist in nature, will quickly disappear from the scene, to be replaced by more diffuse and less ideological religious movements. However, there is every sign that their influence is growing, not abating; similar fundamentalist upsurges, linked both to the United States and local forces of repression, are taking place in countries like South Africa and the Philippines.

The "Moonies," although they have a small membership, have shown a remarkable ability to function in various parts of the globe with maximum effectiveness. CAUSA, the "Confederation of the Associations for the Unification of the Societies of the Americas," is the political arm of the Unification Church which has ties to extreme right-wing organizations, like the World Anti-Communist League, in the Western Hemisphere and around the world. CAUSA's affiliate in the Philippines is the Spiritual Action Movement Foundation, which is headed by Celia Diaz-Laurel, wife of Corazon Aquino's vice president. CAUSA, along with other Moon organizations, sponsors lavish conferences for unassociated academics and religious leaders; these gatherings are very similar whether they are held in Miami or halfway round the world in Japan.

In 1990 the Reverend Moon traveled to Moscow and met with Mikhail Gorbachev. Later that year hundreds of Soviet students were traveling to the United States for "Moonie" indoctrination sessions: they were taught the glories of world unification under a new Asian-American, Protestant-capitalist order. At almost the same moment, in the People's Republic of China, the government approved an investment by the Unification Church of $250 million in a new automobile factory. The Church is particularly adept at moving money, the sources of which are very suspect, to other parts of the world. In the early 1980s the apartheid government of South Africa invested $4.5 million through secret "Moonie" networks so that it could own a substantial interest in *The Washington Times*, which in turn published articles which were very favorable to the South African regime.

The Unification Church and hundreds of other late 20th century manifestations of evangelical Protestantism are not the only religious forces that help to further the spread of authoritarian capitalism. For instance, fundamentalist Islam has been a very handy tool for the neo-fascist, military-dominated regimes of Pakistan, Indonesia, and Turkey as they attempt to discipline and control their populations while proceeding with a very harsh process of modernization. Still, evangelical Christian ministers seem to have special advantages in many parts of the world where they can adapt the U.S. heritage of the "manifest destiny" of capitalism to various local and national contexts. As cheerleaders and entrepreneurs on behalf of fundamentalist Americanism, these ministers all support the "destiny" of global profit-making enterprises. At times, this relationship has even prepared some evangelicals, like Reverends Moon and Robertson, to invent religious mechanisms which can churn out their own profits on a global scale.

The example of the "Moonies," a small but powerful sect, is worth our attention. This is not because the Unification Church is destined to take over the world, nor because it might spawn dozens of imitators anxious to cash in on its unique concentration of economic, religious, and political power in one organization. It is likely that the strange concurrence of the coming of a second Messiah, the machinations of the Korean CIA, and the collection of billions of dollars in unexplained assets is simply too unique to be reproduced by other religious entrepreneurs. It is rather as a metaphor of our times that the Unification Church should be examined, as a crystallization of extreme right-wing authoritarianism that has prospered internationally while various humanistic visions have waned. In one body directed by Reverend Moon, we see the aggressive expansionism of capital flanked by its most important supporting elements, a rigid cultural dogmatism that claims to be universal and a willingness to use imperialistic subversion to achieve its ends. Perhaps this particular manifestation of late 20th century fascism is too "perfect" to be reproduced on a large scale, but it nevertheless points to one of the future paths the capitalist system could take: it represents the terrible synergy of fundamentalist religious certainty, secret service political intrigue and terror, and the relentless search for new ways to produce a profit.

Chapter 19

THE GLOBAL ECONOMY - CAPITALIST VALUES IMPOSED WORLDWIDE

The rapid spread of capitalist institutions across the globe has not been accompanied by a new diffusion of wealth throughout the world. In the past twenty-five years, the overall balance of economic power has shifted more rapidly than ever in favor of the rich countries of the North:

- Just 17% of the world's population lives in the developed industrial countries, yet they collect 82% of the world's income.

- In 1850 - Europe and the United States had a standard of living that was about 50% higher than the rest of the world.

- In 1965 - The U.S., Europe, and Japan had an average per capita income which was 14 times greater than the average for all the rest of the world.

- By 1988 - the per capita income of these rich countries was 23.4 times greater than the rest of the world.

THE GLOBAL ECONOMY- CAPITALIST VALUES IMPOSED WORLDWIDE

The rapid movement of capital around the globe and the continuing internationalization of production in many industries have created many industrial pockets that channel profits back to the owning classes in the richest countries. The export platforms of the Third World, around which congregate the job-hungry poor, are the late 20th century counterparts of the old English and American mill towns. Throughout the world the most exploited people are often young female workers, a fact that brings to mind Marx's analysis of exploitation:

"We have seen that the development of the capitalist mode of production and of the productive power of labor - at once the cause and effect of accumulation - enables the capitalist, with the same outlay of variable capital, to set in action more labour by greater exploitation (extensive or intensive) of each individual labour-power. We have further seen that the capitalist buys with the same capital a greater mass of labour-power, as he progressively replaces skilled laborers with less skilled, mature labour-power by immature, male by female, that of adults by young people and children."

At the end of the 1980s, as ever greater amounts of capital were pouring into the centers of world finance, one might have thought that the capitalist system was working smoothly. After all, the Western countries were rejoicing at the self-destruction of the authoritarian state bureaucracies in the Eastern bloc and trumpeting the victory and further spread of capitalist ideas.

Yet at the same time, the capitalist world system did not look very healthy, for in fact it was threatened by instability and numerous rashly conceived solutions to the problem of establishing an orderly accumulation of money. The United States, in a fit of deregulation, had set loose a maniacal army of speculators and loan sharks who emptied out the assets of U.S. financial institutions, most notably in the $500 billion Savings and Loan scam. The banks of all the industrialized countries were over-investing in commercial real estate after having indulged in a disastrous Third-World lending spree which often favored the most disreputable dictatorships in Asia, the Americas and Africa. Consequently billions of potential consumers in the "undeveloped" world were victimized by indebtedness recklessly incurred on behalf of

"growth," so that they ultimately had little money available to buy the products which the transnational corporations wanted to sell them.

In the 1980s the economic disaster for most of the American countries and almost all of Africa came in the form of a true depression, lower standards of living accompanied by lower production, particularly in industry. The capitalist development of agriculture, one of the few ways available to pay off the foreign debts of the poor countries, added further to the suffering of the world's poorest citizens. Production of basic foodstuffs that are consumable by rural peasants and urban slumdwellers fell sharply as large-scale agro-export capitalism grew. The goods created for the world market did not adequately compensate the large majority of workers, so that the local citizens suffered from worsening diets and an absolute decrease in their daily intake of calories.

The world was witnessing a large-scale restructuring of its economic system, now more capitalist than it had ever been, and many people had to suffer so that the profitability of the major corporations and investors could be restored to new health. Whether this "restoration" of capital has truly reinvigorated the world system is still very much in doubt, but what is very clear is that the North - the Europeans, the European Americans, and the Japanese - have gained mightily at the expense of the South.

This kind of systemized oppression for the sake of profit, which we have identified with Columbus and the conquest of America, must now, more than ever, be understood and analyzed on a world scale. Pressures on industrial workers and agricultural workers in one part of the globe effect laborers in other regions because they are so often producing for the same world markets, for the same transnational corporations and investors. What had once been accomplished by imperialistic armies and colonial structures can now be enforced by "austerity programs" recommended by the International Monetary Fund, which sets the standards by which one country must compete with others in the disciplinary action imposed upon its working classes.

The ruthlessness of competition on the global scale has encouraged the rise of productive states, like South Korea, which are rather frightening models of future development. But even these Newly Industrializing Countries cannot be assured of continued success, even if they succeed in muzzling their restive citizens. These "economic miracle" countries have been slowing under the strain that has debilitated other parts of the globe. By early 1990 the Korean rates of growth had dropped to around 6%, about half of their levels in the mid 1980s; suddenly the nation had a trade debt instead of a surplus. The U.S., in trying to curb its own incredible trade deficit, stopped granting some of the special favors that had encouraged South Korean exports. And at the same time, there were other Asian countries competing to fill the shoes of the Korean low-cost producers. So when South Korean workers wanted to raise their miserable wages and shorten their long workweeks, their capitalist-militarist rulers struck back immediately with government force. At this point, both their political stability and profit-making prowess have been put in doubt.

The South Korean model was breaking down in the face of the more potent Asian force, the overwhelming influence of Japanese capital. Japan, even as it was making large investments in Europe and the U.S., was putting its largest amounts of foreign investment capital into the development of Asian industry. The biggest boom country of Asia in the late 1980s and early 1990s was Thailand, which experienced phenomenal growth rates like South Korea had once known: 13.2% in 1988, 12.2% in 1989, 10.5% in 1990. The Japanese invested nearly half of the $8.2 billion dollars in foreign capital that flowed into Thailand in 1989, much of it in the production of Japanese brand automobiles - by 1992 Japanese officials are confident that 300,000 Thai workers will be assembling their autos. The United States once had been the biggest investor in South East Asia, but by 1989 Japan was investing seven times as much as the Americans.

If South Korea had an advantage in the mid 1980s, when its laborers took home only 1/10th of what autoworkers earned in the advanced industrial countries, then the Thai equation looked even more advantageous in 1990: an average Thai auto worker earned $200 a month, just about what a Japanese worker would earn in a single day. On this basis, the Korean corporate networks or chaebol, as powerful as they are at home, may have trouble competing with the Japanese auto giants. With low wage labor, the Japanese are setting up factories "that look like flashbacks to the 1930s," using old equipment that will not compete with the ultra-modern robotics being installed in Japan. One business magazine, *The Far Eastern Economic Review*, pointed out that low wages were not the only advantage for Thailand: compared to the rest of developing Asia's already abysmal standards, Thailand had "minimal industrial controls relating to safety, health, pollution, and worker welfare." Helping to enforce these conditions is an anti-democratic military regime.

South Korea may be caught in the middle, having invested part-way in more sophisticated technology but unable to compete with the most modern of Japanese plants; at the same time, it cannot compete with the lower cost labor in Thailand which is tied into the advantages of a Japanese production system that now serves and is served by almost all of Southeast Asia, including Malaysia, Indonesia, Singapore, and the Philippines. The Mitsubishi car that sells in Canada under the name of Chrysler is really assembled in Thailand with parts contributed from factories in other low-wage Asian countries. So powerful is the unpredictable growth which is underway in East Asia that even Malaysia, not so long ago the archtypical Asian producer of raw commodities with its rubber and mining exports, has now become primarily a manufacturing exporter:

Malaysian exports	1970	1989
primary commodities	78.4%	32.3%
manufacturing	7.6%	54.7%

THE BEAUTY OF CAPITALISM

As we witness the frenetic movement of capital from country to country and attempt to make some sense out of the proceedings, it is worth reflecting on some simple observations of capitalist behavior. For one, a company like Mitsubishi, with its productive nodes in various parts of Asia, is typical of many other Japanese, American and European transnational corporations, which have prepared themselves to operate efficiently in the ever more homogenous world market. These giant companies are complex organizations capable of concentrating on minute details which will give them an advantage over their rivals. Yet all of their brain power and planning ignores countless facets of human life; it is focused on a single concept: producing the highest possible return to one's investors.

This is the beauty of capitalism: it is built upon the extremely simple premise of creating private profit before considering any other human need. All the competitors, whether they play fairly or not (this is really not expected), are playing the same game. The single-mindedness of capitalism, once epitomized by such "Robber Barons" as John D. Rockefeller and E.H. Harriman, is now systemitized into the logic of the transnational corporations. They operate with a high degree of rationality and purposefulness that is rarely matched in other human endeavors. And, one must admit, this activity, though it certainly does not represent the full flowering of human potential, has created a degree of wealth and productivity previously unknown to humankind.

On the other hand, because maximization of profit has always been the name of the game, corporations are willing to use coercive methods to achieve their aims, just like the entrepreneurs who preceded them in earlier stages of capitalist expansion. Furthermore, when these modern entities operate in what were once the colonies, and now constitute the Third World, they have had little trouble in integrating different modes of production into the world system. The banks, trading companies, and corporations at the top of the world pyramid of ownership do not need to control every operation in the world production and distribution scheme - they need only say: "bring me such-and-such at this price, or less." At that point small foreign traders, or medium-sized national companies, or even local state-sponsored entities will endeavor to deliver the resource wanted or to market the good produced in the corporate factory.

In this way different kinds of economic exploitation, in different places, are appropriate at any one time in capitalist development. For instance, in the 19th century, at the same time that the working class expanded in Europe and provided the labor for burgeoning industrial capitalism, in other parts of the world there were still examples of classic pillage-and-burn accumulation, the "primitive capitalism" of modern day conquistadors. What was Cecil Rhodes but a sort of 19th century Columbus, or more to the point, a Cortez or a Pizarro, when he led a small army up into the middle of Africa, a long journey of conquest which created his own "empire" within the British Empire?

Just one hundred years ago, the Queen of the world's most advanced industrial country gave Rhodes permission to set up the British South Africa Company on the same model that had served the Dutch so admirably almost 300 years before, when South Africa was just an outpost for ships of the Dutch East India Company. The profits to be gained from both mineral production and plantation agriculture in Africa proved significant enough for the British army to send in forces to protect the booty gathered up in Rhodes' imperialistic excursion, as he journeyed from South Africa to his new fiefdom in Rhodesia. Rhodes' adventures, much like the other conquistadors', were characterized by systematized theft which shipped out a variety of plunder; in almost every region through which Rhodes trampled there was something to be seized or extracted that was useful in Britain's home markets.

The Queen of England was sent an anxious query from King Lobengula, leader of the Amandebele people in Rhodesia:

"Your majesty, what I want to know from you is if people can be bought at any price... Your majesty, what I want to know from you is: why do your people kill me?"

The king's other message, which easily could have been voiced by an American monarch concerning the Spanish invasion 400 years earlier, was addressed to his own people:

"The white man will never cease following us while we have gold in our possession, for gold is what white men prize above all things. Collect all my gold...and carry it to the white men."

King Lobengula's willingness to part with his gold was insufficient. Today, one hundred years after his demise at the hands of the English, it is still true that, providing that profit margins are high, the advanced capitalist states and their modern corporations have both the ability and predisposition to "do business" with "less advanced" colleagues in the rest of the world: with the Apartheid system in South Africa, with a police state in Korea, with "death squads" in Guatemala, with the world's worst polluters in the Brazilian industrial belt, with certain kinds of outdated factories in ultra-low wage Thailand, or with a socially backward fiefdom in Saudi Arabia.

RATIONAL CORPORATIONS AND GLOBAL MADNESS

Perhaps readers are wondering why they are being assailed by these confusing tidbits about modern investment and corporate activity in Korea and Thailand and Southern Africa. Are the citizens of the North supposed to shoulder the burden of guilt for everything that happens in the world? (Well, maybe...)

Actually, the intent here is to make the reader question the rationality of the capitalist system. It is difficult for someone who works hard every day - whether as a machinist, a secretary, a middle manager, or an engineer - within a large and seemingly rational structure of a North American, European, or Japanese corporation, to question the very organization that seems so productive and efficient, the business entity that is envied by the rest of the world. What is difficult to comprehend, perhaps, is that even though the modern corporation dedicates itself so steadily to rational production and distribution of its goods and services, even though its top managers stay finely attuned to the bottom line and the computation of profit margins, outside the corporation the world is not so rational. In fact, what seems like ultimate attention to the details of profitability and scientific management within the corporation may, when seen in the light of worldwide economic events, reveal itself to be naked greed, a destructive force unleased by a monomaniacal love for gold or money.

It is evident now that the 1980s were a decade of "business worship" in the advanced capitalist countries and especially in the United States. Ordinary citizens, many with little money to invest, were buying up countless books on finance, money, "success," and "power," as if they, too, could be happy capitalists. Business language and the ethics of self-aggrandizement pervaded the popular culture, as people were told by pop-psychologists to pursue love and fame, family and individual happiness as if they were things that could be bought and sold and hustled by the strongest bidder.

These same citizens were to wake up in the 1990s and realize that, in the United States and many other parts of the world, the "money madness" had led to social disaster. While millions of middle class citizens had indulged themselves in consumer debt, the bankers and corporate directors and their government representatives, the people who were supposed to be expertly guiding the engines of modern capital, went on a rampage of wasteful speculation that simply destroyed trillions of dollars in assets. One debacle alone, the looting of the U.S. Savings and Loan industry, is expected to cost at least half a trillion dollars; the instability of the U.S. commercial banking sector is likely to require similar infusions of public funds. There were many other ways for those with the MBAs to practice their grasp of capitalist theory, both inside and outside the United States:

• Laundering hundreds of billions of dollars worth of drug money

• Continuing to promote a worldwide armaments industry, to the the detriment of most Third World countries

• Imposing a debt burden upon Third World countries which cannot be paid back to First World lenders

• over-investing in real estate of all kinds, but especially in commercial office buildings, the monuments which contemporary corporate capital builds in honor of itself

Our list could keep expanding, but the point should be evident enough: vast resources were wasted by a so-called "rational" economic system because it could not find productive ways to employ them. Meanwhile millions of U.S. citizens and billions of world citizens who would have benefited from the useful deployment of that capital sank further into poverty. U.S. capitalists were not especially guilty compared to others, for the phenomenon was worldwide. One of the more hideous details of how the system "worked" concerns the methods employed by the international banks.

In the 1970s, U.S., Swiss, British, and other major capitalist banking centers had established or modernized active branch banks all over the world. One of their primary goals was to enlarge their "private banking departments" and entice the local capitalists, dictators, and oil functionaries of Third World countries to deposit their capital assets in First World accounts. As the New York Times business pages informed us in 1989:

> *"Private international banking departments have long accepted and sometimes actively sought the deposits of foreigners looking to move hundreds of billions of dollars away from weak economies, or seeking to evade tax or currency laws or hide their money for a variety of reasons."*

The confidentiality and evasiveness of "private banking" created a labyrinth of secret ploys for moving the money of rich individuals from country to country. The poor countries were at a loss to control this movement, called "flight capital," which often deprived them of the resources necessary for internal development, modernization, and the amelioration of the poverty of their poorest citizens. The Bank of International Settlements in Basel, Switzerland estimated, with a very conservative figure that did not include illegal transactions, that $170 billion escaped from 10 Latin American countries between 1978 and 1987. Economist Arthur MacEwan estimates that the figure was much higher and that rich Mexicans alone took about $100 billion out of their economy, an amount large enough to pay off their foreign debt.

In late 1991, the most scandalous revelations of international banking involved BCCI, the Bank of Credit and Commerce International of Luxembourg, which had once been the world's 5th largest private bank. The BCCI, which all of a sudden could not locate at least $30 billion in assets, seemed to have been involved in all sorts of international crime and intrigue - massive drug money laundering, secret CIA accounts, and financing for Arab terrorists were among its specialties. The BCCI achieved many of its aims by making blatant payoffs to some of the most respected financiers and politicians in the United States and Europe;

this made it easy to appear respectable itself, as when it bought control of the largest bank holding company in Washington, D.C., First American Bankshares.

Private banking has flourished because it has been incredibly lucrative for the banks, which had no shortage of customers who were intent on looting their own countries and becoming upstanding members of the international bourgeoisie. The Marcos family of the Philippines, who invested billions of dollars in U.S. real estate, engaged in some of the more blatant acts of thievery, but their example was followed by thousands of more discreet players; the activities of the latter were regarded as perfectly acceptable because, as one financial analyst revealed, the profits were so handsome:

"Rich investors are willing to pay high fees and accept low yields. Thus, a bank's return on equity for private banking can exceed 100 per cent."

The chumminess of secret personal contacts across the continents was enhanced by technological developments in the computerized movement of money from account to account. The dizzying speed of transactions opened up new business opportunities:

"The growth of flight capital in the 1970s laid the framework for money laundering in the 1980s."

"Money laundering," of course, was the way that illicit drug money amounting to hundreds of billions of dollars found its way through the channels of the private banking system. How was one to distinguish the "dirty" money - from Panamanians who served the Colombian cocaine trade, and Pakistani generals who served the heroin trade, and North American businessmen who invested in the sale of "crack" to ghetto children - from any other international deposits?

What was "legitimate," in any case? The established rule of international investment was that there were no rules, except to protect free trade and the steady flow of profits. In the past capitalist powers have fought wars in order to protect the rights of private investors to trade in drugs, most notably the Opium Wars of the 19th century which Britain waged against China so that its trading companies could sell the vast quantities of opium they were cultivating in India to Chinese consumers. Some people in the United States were sympathetic to the British and disdainful of a Chinese society which tried to resist the creation of millions of drug addicts among its citizenry. John Quincy Adams, sixth President of the United States, recognized that the Chinese were lacking in certain Western virtues; he gave a lecture on the subject, explaining that the "churlish" Chinese were just asking for a beating at the hands of the English:

"The moral obligation of commercial intercourse between nations is founded entirely, exclusively, upon the Christian precept to love your neighbor as yourself... but China, not being a Christian nation, its inhabitants do not consider themselves bound by the Christian concept, to love their neighbor as themselves... this is a churlish and unsocial system... the fundamental principle of the Chinese system is anti-commercial... It is time that this enormous outrage upon the rights of human nature, and upon the first principles of the rights of nations, should cease."

This fine exercise in rhetoric, with its high notes linking Christianity and Commerce, was Adams' way of heralding British imperialism and anticipating the day when the young offspring of Britain would itself be able to assume the mantle of world empire.

Chapter 20

NEW WORLD ORDER, SAME OLD EMPIRE

*"The world is divided into two groups of people: the Christian
anti-communists, and the others."*

- John Foster Dulles, U.S. Secretary of State in the 1950s

For 45 years the war waged by North against South, by advanced capitalism against the rest of the world, took place under the banner of a holy war against Communism. In the 1990s, with the Cold War over, a new era began:

1989-90 - The United States invaded Panama, sending a unmistakable signal to Latin America and the Caribbean that it planned to retain control over the affairs of the Western Hemisphere.

1990-91 - The United States and its allies bombed Iraq and invaded the Middle East with over half a million troops in order to reassert their control over the world's oil supplies. The message to the South was clear: conform to the economic and political requirements of the capitalist world system.

NEW WORLD ORDER, SAME OLD EMPIRE

For the past five decades the United States has often resorted to force in order to impose its will on both small and large countries. Sometimes the targets of aggression were uncooperative nations ruled by small-time bullies, like Noreiga in Panama and Hussein in Iraq, who had once been the recipients of U.S. favoritism. Other victims were "innocent" democracies attempting to chart an independent course. Certainly the United States and other countries often believed that these were confrontations between the "free world" and "Communism," but there was something else going on, too. The United States was promoting the natural propensity of capitalism to keep expanding, and it did so by maintaining and extending its dominance, both economic and military, over most of the world. This is known as imperialism, and the following list touches upon just a few of the imperialist actions that were necessary for re-establishing capitalist hegemony:

1945-1990 - The United States began the long-term military occupation of Germany and Japan, controlling the direction of their economic and political development in order to negate the dangerous imperialist rivalries that had torn the advanced capitalist North apart. The U.S. presence in Europe through NATO allowed it to set up numerous secret networks which undermined the democratic institutions of individual countries; for instance, the support of the military regime of the Colonels in Greece and the long-term presence of an underground "Gladio" network in Italy.

1950-1990 - After the Korean War, South Korea came under the control of the United States and became a model for a new style of energetic capitalist development under a neo-fascist system of disciplining labor and limiting ideological debate.

1953 - The Central Intelligence Agency staged a coup in Iran in order to keep a democratic government from nationalizing the holdings of the global oil corporations. The Shah was set up as a despotic ruler whose secret police had one of the worst human rights records in the world.

1954-1990 - A CIA coup in Guatemala eliminated the only truly democratic government which the nation ever had; it unleashed a 35 year reign of terror that protected the rich oligarchy and American corporate investments; Guatemalan death squads became the model for imposing capitalist discipline throughout Latin America.

1964 - The CIA-supported coup in Brazil removed another left-leaning democratic government and created the South American model for fast-paced industrial development with mountains of debt supplied by First World banks, all under the watch of the right-wing dictatorship of the generals.

1965 - The CIA-assisted military coup in Indonesia ended in the slaughter of between 600,000 and 1,000,000 civilians suspected of leftist associations; it resulted in a permanent East Asian model of friendly economic development backed by an authoritarian Islamic military government.

1965-1975 - The U.S. made a commitment of 500,000 troops to a large-scale war against a national liberation movement in Vietnam. The U.S. did not "win" but almost completely destroyed the country; two to three million people were killed, a discouraging message to any other country which might have thought of breaking out of its place in the world system.

1973 - Chile's experiment with a mixed democratic socialist economy was brought to an abrupt end by a U.S. economic boycott and a CIA plot. Then, under General Pinochet, Chile became a model in the effective application of austerity and terror.

1979-1990 - Nicaragua staged a popular revolution almost next door to the United States, but was gradually ground down to utter poverty and desperation by a U.S. economic blockade and a CIA-led Contra War. The revolution of the Salvadoran peasants was stopped brutally in its tracks, though not defeated.

1981-1990 - The U.S. tried to practice "constructive engagement" with South Africa, rather than punish it for its system of apartheid; simultaneously the U.S. encouraged South Africa as it waged successful wars against the anti-capitalist black African governments in neighboring Angola and Mozambique.

THE RESTORATION OF GLOBAL POWER

The U.S. success at extending the world-wide reach of capitalism had an earlier precedent. Once before, with the rise and rapid development of industrial capitalism in the 19th century, the white Northerners of Europe had acquired both the means and the motivations to integrate the whole world into their economic system. They overran most of the globe in a very short time, virtually completing the process of colonization that had begun centuries earlier in the Americas:

Percentage of the Earth's Surface Controlled by Europeans

1800 - 35%	1878 - 67%	1914 - 84.4%

But then the system destroyed itself. The two World Wars and the escape of the Soviet Union from the world system spoiled the systematic march of industrial and monopoly capital. The spread of capitalist imperialism in the 19th century generated serious rivalries for domination of different parts of the world, so that the newcomers, Germany and Japan, were determined to establish their own Empires equal or superior to the English, U.S., and French models. When the whole process degenerated into history's greatest militarist disaster, the capitalist North was fragmented and weak, leaving the United States as the dominant country which would have to attempt to put the pieces of empire back together again.

If the capitalist system was to be re-established to its pre-World War I proportions - this time with the integration of the Third World, not just as suppliers of raw materials but also as low wage industrial producers - then the United States, as leader of the capitalist powers, needed to employ various methods. Sometimes it asserted its power in a fairly benign fashion, through the largesse of foreign aid or the targeted investment strategies of private companies. At other moments, the U.S. required a pretext for the reconquest of the numerous countries who sought some degree of independence. The Cold War, the fight against Communism, became both the justification and the means for installing a whole series of semi-fascist militarist dictatorships which were friendly and responsive to U.S. and European demands. By the end of the 1980s, some of these militarist regimes were changing into extremely weak pseudo- democracies - the Philippines and Pakistan, for instance - which were thoroughly at the service of the international corporate and banking apparatus and willing to impose severe austerity measures on their people.

At the beginning of the 1990s, the invasions of Panama and Iraq signaled a new era. All those actions taken in the previous 45 years by the United States, whether bolstering the industrial world or punishing the Third World, were taken in the name of anti-Communism. In retrospect, we realize that the Soviet Union never had been able to create a strong counter-Empire (Ronald Reagan's so-called "Evil Empire") that could effectively answer the aggressions and manipulations of the capitalist empire builders. The shell the Soviets built around themselves and Eastern Europe was generally protective and utterly weak. On the one rare occasion when the Soviet Union ventured just outside its borders, in Afghanistan, it failed miserably.

The collapse of the Soviet system allowed the U.S. to move quickly to re-establish forms of imperialist control without the need for the rhetoric of anti-Communism. Its allies in Europe and Japan, although reluctant to engage in outright invasions of other countries, were happy to have some U.S. troops removed from their own countries. In 1990, these countries complied with U.S. wishes and passed resolutions presented at the United Nations that gave the U.S. the "green light" to launch an important offensive against Iraq.

Saddam Hussein, the thoroughly undesirable dictator of Iraq, made a serious miscalculation when he invaded Kuwait. He was looking for large sums of oil money to help pay off the huge debts incurred in the long, bloody war with Iran, and he was angry that Kuwait had reneged on its agreement with Saudi Arabia and Iraq to put limits on oil production. Hussein, like Panama's Noriega, had been a long-term CIA asset, and had received considerable U.S. aid and encouragement throughout the 1980s while he made war against Iran. But by August 1990 he was expendable and no longer served the interests of the North. British journalist John Pilger suggested during the course of the Iraqi war that President Bush ought to be one person who could recall the special relationship between the United States and the local tyrant:

> *"As former director of the CIA, Bush will know... that the CIA virtually put Saddam and his Ba'athist fascists in power; that a CIA directed campaign oversaw the slaughter of the Iraqi left: socialists, trade unionists, teachers, journalists."*

Saddam Hussein's bloody practices, ignored for so many years, were suddenly discovered by the U.S. State Department and the corporate media and he became "another Hitler," the target of a "just war." Saddam provided a handy pretext for the United States to invade the Middle East with over 400,000 troops, more than it had kept in Europe during the Cold War, almost as many as it committed to Vietnam. When had any country ever moved so many forces around the world and then been deterred from putting them to use?

Despite efforts of the Arab world, the Europeans, the Japanese, the Russians, and the entire apparatus of the United Nations, peace negotiations were not taken seriously by the United States. Both the Pentagon and the New York Times, two preeminent representatives of the U.S. power structure, spoke openly of wanting to "take Hussein out" by proceeding with war. Before the war began (and before the average American citizen succumbed to the anesthetizing effects of patriotism) the underlying intention for the U.S. intervention was clear even to its own citizens; when interviewed by television news reporters they regularly identified the culprit: "BIG OIL."

From 1928 to 1972, oil in the Middle East had been controlled by the fabled seven sisters - Exxon, Shell, Mobil, British Petroleum, Gulf, Texaco, and Chevron:

> *"As late as 1972, the seven international majors were still producing 91% of Middle East crude oil and 77% of the Free World's supply outside of the U.S."*

In 1990, more than one hundred years after the Rockefeller monopoly had recognized the absolutely key role which oil would play in capitalist industrial development, the world was still tremendously dependent on oil for its prosperity. The invasion of the Middle East by the United States was the way that the North guaranteed its control over the world's largest deposits of oil; between 50 to 60 per cent of the world oil reserves lie in the Middle East.

NEW WORLD DISORDER

The military-industrial complex of the United States is confronted with intense competition from superior industrial production in Europe and Japan, not to mention cheaper competition from the rest of the world. Rather than meeting these challenges by the painful process of restructuring the U.S. economy, it is tempting to rely on the maintenance of the old war machine and its attendant industries. During the Gulf War, George Bush and his colleagues thought it was possible for the U.S. to assume the role of a centurion nation on behalf of the other advanced capitalist economies, like Germany and Japan. It was time to play "Rent-a-Cop," and the State Department was not shy about telling the major capitalist nations as well as the oil sheiks that it would present them with part of the bill for the Gulf War. The way was open for the U.S. to send its legions forth to remote parts of the world in order to impose "economic peace," that is, to force compliance with capitalist priorities on any upstart nations around the world. U.S. Army Chief of Staff, General Carl Vuono, anticipated this role in April of 1990, when he wrote in the magazine *Seapower*:

> *"Because the U.S. is a global power with vital interests that must be protected throughout an increasingly turbulent world, we must look beyond the European continent and consider other threats to our national security."*

This was the reality behind President Bush's proclamation of "a New World Order." For the U.S. was not just "a global power," it was the only global power. And because of this, there was a purpose behind the uncompromising bombardment of Iraq that went beyond returning control of the oil fields to capitalist investors. There was a message to the world that was stated perfectly by Joshua Muravchik of the conservative American Enterprise Institute on the pages of *The New York Times*:

> *"The Gulf war marks the dawning of the Pax Americana... During the past two years...Soviet power has imploded and a bipolar world has become unipolar. A global rush toward democracy and free markets has spelled a huge victory for America on the ideological plane. Now, in the Gulf War, our ideological supremacy is being matched by a demonstration of America's refurbished military capability."*

Pax Americana, Pax Britannica, Pax Romana - these are euphemistic names for stable empires whose hegemony goes unchallenged. In this sense, when George Bush and his ideologists tried to describe "the new world order," they were talking with fuzzy nostalgia about a benevolent and prosperous American empire that never really existed.

The real prospects for a rosy era of Pax Americana seem doubtful. Three serious obstacles confront the dream of U.S. manifest destiny and the idea that U.S.-style capitalism will triumph worldwide:

- The economic performance of Japan and Germany and their international business networks is clearly superior; these two, the real capitalist powers, will not be willing to remain subservient in military and diplomatic matters which until now have been controlled by the United States.

- We should remember that countries like Spain and Britain, which had the opportunity to exercise military control over the world system in the past, degenerated as they tried to maintain their empires through ruthless and brutal methods. Do we need to look any farther than the U.S. role in Central America to realize that U.S. imperialism can be equally malignant?

- The United States no longer has the capacity to intervene in the affairs of the rest of the world. Forty-five years of international militarism have contributed to the disintegration of many economic and social institutions in the United States. In the face of its domestic inadequacies, it would be suicidal for the United States to keep pursuing imperial adventures.

Chapter 21

THE WORLD SYSTEM LOOKS THE SAME

The Capitalist Pattern of Extracting Wealth from the World in the Late 20th Century

1. Investment capital is put forward by the rich, the transnational corporations, and the international banks.

2. This capital funds corporate subsidiaries and businesses which extract the wealth of the South by whatever means are necessary.

3. Vast profits are realized, further enriching the corporate giants and bourgeois families, but also leaving room for emerging capitalist entities which are particularly inventive or especially ruthless.

4. In order to enforce this process of accumulation, systems of organized violence, including armies and police forces, are required - billions of people must be coerced into working at low wages.

5. Since the creation of a worldwide working class means the subjugation of the "coloreds" of the South to the "whites" of the North, the ideology of racism is being revived.

6. In order to keep the oppressed from rebelling successfully, local elites, including militarists and managers, must align themselves with the forces of capital.

7. The whole system needs justification. For those at the top, both North and South, the rewards of power and the consumer culture are often sufficient. The compliance of the majority of workers cannot be maintained by pure force; a cultural survival mechanism, such as an "enthusiastic religion" which is compatible with capitalism and authoritarianism, is very useful.

8. The rapacious waste of natural resources for short-term profit is exhausting the earth and its capacity to maintain life; meanwhile the North is transferring its technologies of global pollution to the South under conditions that will only destroy the environment more quickly.

The methods of conquest have hardly changed in 500 years.

THE WORLD SYSTEM LOOKS THE SAME

The list of eight capitalist characteristics simply restates the pattern of economic domination which we linked to the enterprise of Columbus at the beginning of the book. Although the capitalist system has developed fully from the seeds that mercantilist capitalism planted 500 years ago in America, the means used to enforce global control have not changed very much. We have witnessed the success of imperialism - or we could say, to the defender of the capitalism system who does not care for the "imperialist" label, that we have seen the inevitable superiority, sometimes regrettably harsh, of capitalist economic and political institutions as they spread around the world.

The problem for those who defend the current capitalist world structure is to reconcile their vision of prosperity with the reality found outside the advanced Northern countries. The picture of the capitalist system that emerged from the 1980s offered these grim realities:

- the extreme discrepancy in wealth between North and South, and within each area, between the fortunes of rich and poor
- the extreme degree of pauperization, famine, and terror that have accompanied global "modernization"
- the lack of functioning democratic institutions in the South which can withstand the overwhelming manipulative power of the North
- the inability of capitalist technology to grapple successfully with the overwhelming threats it has caused to world ecology
- the new uncertainty about leadership and cohesion among the advanced capitalist nations themselves, where both financial systems and political legitimacy are very much in question

THE RETURN TO RACISM

Of all the cultural signposts that speak of uncertainty and desperation, among all the markers that designate what is North and what is South, none is so frightening as the return to open racism on the part of the rich Northerners.

"Humanity is thus faced with a new question. If the present road of development continues, the North-South contradiction will invariably become more and more explosive, thereby engendering, among other things, an intensified aggressive racism in the countries of developed capitalism, of which the prejudice against the Third World is only a precursor."
-Samir Amin, *Eurocentrism*

With the arrival of 1992, Europe celebrates the progress of its economic and political unification as it coincides with the 500th anniversary of the European conquest of America. The celebration of Columbus also salutes the concept of "Western Civilization" and the invention of Eurocentrism, which attributes universal superiority to the culture of Europe because it managed to impose itself on the rest of the world. And, as the North tries to maintain a Eurocentric conception of the world, it is returning to the comforts of racism, the dehumanizing thought process which insulates the sensibilities of the owning classes, and the owning countries, from the realities of systematic poverty and oppression. The world is not moving into a post-industrial age, but simply transferring industry from the high wage areas to the low wage ones of the Third World. These new industrial areas are inhabited by people with skins of a different color, which allows for the rehabilitation of racism, the most convenient ideology for separating the haves from the have-nots.

It is worth recalling the first impressions of Columbus upon encountering the Indians:

"They are a very loving race and without covetousness...there is no better country nor better people in the world."

Within three years, when Columbus and his men were intent on forcing the Indians to be their slaves, the description of the new-found people had turned to vilification and loathing. Their historian, Oviedo, revealed the new image of the Indians:

"...people by nature idle and vicious, doing little work"

This anger on the part of whites, when they cannot tolerate the fact that the oppressed races do not willingly accept the dehumanizing processes of "western civilization," is still alive in the 20th century, and not just in such obvious places as South Africa, Guatemala, and the United States. In France, Germany, and Italy, neo-nationalist and neo-nazi political parties have been forming, and they all vilify the "blacks," an all-purpose term for the people from the South and the Third World. The revived racism of the late 20th century might sometimes look like a matter of isolated incidents involving frustrated elements of society - unemployed autoworkers in Detroit killed a Chinese man whom they had mistaken for a Japanese; poor Southern Italians living in Northern Italy set fire to the cars of North African "extra-communitarians" while the latter were sleeping inside; disgruntled white youths in Germany stalked and murdered Turkish "guestworkers" and South African refugees.

In reality, the acts of whites from the less privileged classes had been encouraged by the overall mood of the ruling classes, especially in the U.S., where the Reagan and Bush administrations dismantled civil rights protections for people of color at the same time that the economic plight of Black and Hispanic families worsened considerably. A conservative shift of thought was taking place in most developed countries, especially in the U.S. and Britain, and to a smaller extent in the rest of Europe: the upper classes were anxious to control a larger share of the surplus value created by labor so they decreased wages and benefits, increased rents and interest rates, and began to dismantle the public sector. This change was coinciding with the economic reality outside the advanced economies: there has been a conversion, a transfer of workshops to the poorer countries of the world. Most electronic goods, a great many automobiles and heavy industry products, increasing quantities of processed foods and export crops, and the usual stream of raw materials, some of them already processed, now come from the periphery of the system.

Throughout the world we have a newly emerging network of industrial exploitation joining the already extensive and brutal system of agricultural factories. (Or should we say that industrial plantations are being set up alongside the agricultural ones?) How does one justify this harsh regime? Why not, like Columbus, engender distrust and disdain for the different racial group? Or, like, 19th century industrialists, create contempt for the working classes and glorify the upper class through a belief in Social Darwinism?

Best of all, why not combine these two prejudices? Now the world's working classes, more clearly than ever before, are also the different racial groups. This provides a valuable pretext for reconstructing the legacy of discrimination and a sort of "upper class consciousness" under the new regime of capital. As the racism which is contained within Eurocentrism becomes clearly evident once again, it should not be confused with ethnocentrism, the attachment to one's own culture and habits that all nations and peoples share. Racism is characteristic of conquering societies which have reason to keep the "other," the conquered, in conditions of subjection and degradation. Racism requires a system of social beliefs that denies the humanity of the oppressed.

Outside of Europe, in all other parts of the world until 1945, the dominant capitalist countries had little compunction about exercising extreme racist behavior in the pursuit of their economic objectives: England in India, the Caribbean and Africa; France in Africa and Indochina; Holland in In-donesia; Germany in Southwest Africa; the United States with its own African-American, Indian, Hawaiian and Hispanic populations as well as with the peoples of Latin America and the Caribbean. Japan, though not a "white European country," still practiced a nearly analogous kind of capitalist racism in its conquest of Korea and China. The attempt to downplay such open racism and make some amends, both in real legal and social contexts and in more ephemeral public discourse, was only evident on a world scale from about 1945 to 1975, a brief thirty year period which coincided with the national wars of liberation in the Third World, the end of the old styles of colonialism, and the era of desegregation and civil rights movements in the United States. The "good behavior" of the capitalist core countries coincided with the struggle to win the Cold War; the semi-dormancy of open racism coincided with the need of the West to combat the East in the battle for the hearts and minds of potential revolutionaries in every part of the globe.

From our current vantage point we can see that we have passed through a period of transition, from a world colonial system controlled by Europe, the U.S., and Japan, to an integrated international manufacturing system with headquarters in the same places. We could say that the Second Half of the Industrial Revolution has taken, or is taking, place; that the world's citizens have been convincingly proletarianized; and that racism, from the point of view of the North, is a fine way to justify the continued oppression of the South.

If we look back to the period when the North created its own working classes, we will recall that average people resisted mightily. The proletariats created in the 19th and early 20th centuries fought to resist their subjection to capitalist requirements and they won some important victories - concessions to the value of their humanity - in the welfare states of the advanced industrial nations.

Why should the non-white populations of the earth accept their adjustment to the requirements of capital any more easily than the original industrial proletariat did, especially when they live so far from the places where the fruits of their productive activities are enjoyed? The multitudes of the South are sure to keep rebelling against the international regime as they continue to become more aware of their exploitation at the hands of the Northerners. The North, on the other hand, needs a way to convince the world's majority that they should have faith in the mysterious goodness behind the Invisible Hand, that they too have a place in a universal system, and that their suffering and labor will eventually be rewarded.

Chapter 22

SAVING OUR PLANET

- Smog from factories and automobiles threatens the health of all the world's major cities.

- Acid rain drifts out of industrial centers to kill forests and other vegetation.

- Carbon dioxide produced by burning fossil fuels and forests warms up the earth's atmosphere.

- Chlorofluorohydrocarbons and other chemical products destroy the earth's ozone layer.

- The world's forests are disappearing, clean water is getting scarce, and the world's deserts are spreading.

- Nuclear power, the energy solution offered by transnational corporate technology, creates even more opportunities for ecological disaster - through warfare, accidents, and the unsolved problem of waste storage.

"We do not support an Amazonian development policy that favors large entrepreneurs who exploit and massacre workers and destroy nature."

"We demand a development policy that favors workers and not the large estate owners and the multinationals."

-The Brazilian National Rubber Tappers' Council, 1985

SAVING OUR PLANET

Today, rubber tappers in remote Brazil can understand that the future of their children and grandchildren is tied to the willingness of people worldwide to comprehend the global picture. There are many poor working people like the rubber tappers throughout the Americas and the Third World, who recognize human and ecological exploitation when they see it and organize themselves to stop it. Their clear-sightedness and their ability to organize in the face of repressive violence are often in stark contrast with the oblivious complacency of those in the North who are busy consuming the world's wealth.

In recent years, the capitalist ability to produce wealth has been more and more overshadowed by the possibility of an apocalyptic future. The conditions which push us toward global non-viability are the product of the "natural" growth and dissemination of capitalist technology, meaning the arrival of the Industrial Revolution to the Third World. Industrial capitalism could be seen, from the earth's perspective, as a parasitical human vine that has spread over the whole surface of the globe, has sucked out fossil fuels at every opportunity, and then has released every possible kind of contaminant and poison. In the Third World, industrialization is accompanied, as it was in the First World, by unemployment and displacement of human inhabitants, who then are pushed by circumstance to destroy the marginal farming areas and wilderness around them. Global water supplies, forest reserves, and air quality suffer all the more from this secondary effect.

Although it might be possible for the corporations of the North to agree to limit the damage caused by their own national transportation and energy systems (for instance, Western Europeans have made some progress toward controlling acid rain), they will not be so constrained in the rest of the world. In the Third World, profitability depends on lack of controls: unlimited exploitation of labor and the natural environment go hand in hand. If anything, the increasing competition of the factories in the developing world with those in the North will mean increasing pressure on the advanced countries to lower their pollution standards as well as their wages. This is already in evidence in the United States; a kind of "Latin-Americanization" of the U.S. economy took place under the Reagan and Bush administrations, which in the 1980s chose to abandon many environmental protection programs while also undermining programs dedicated to the health and safety of workers.

As the 1990s began, the working and middle classes of Western Europe were partially protected from the consequences of this new wave of capitalist expansion. Their traditions of social democracy and welfare capitalism, and the heritage of old democratic socialist values, had originated in their peoples' response to the first wave of industrial capitalism. These anti-capitalist movements did not succeed in replacing capitalism, but they did manage to enforce serious limitations on the options of the capitalist class, while insuring many adequate safeguards for the health, safety, and welfare of the majority.

Now the social democrats have to engage in some new thinking. For most of the last 500 years, "exploiting nature" has been encouraged by everyone in the capitalist countries. Until very recently, even those who were outraged at the exploitation of human lives in the service of profit-making activities seldom saw any wrong in the unrestrained use of natural resources, thereby "exploiting" nature's abundance in creative ways which harnessed energy and manufactured new goods. This seemed the very essence of being human: to conceive of something that made life better, more interesting or comfortable and then to attempt, through consciously applied work of body and mind, to make the new object.

This European tendency to exploit the opportunities offered by nature never seemed so benign to the original inhabitants of the Americas, who not only lost their lives but also forfeited established patterns of land use and agriculture to the destructive tendencies of mining and plantation enterprises. By now, however, it is also becoming clear to some people in the advanced countries that the fruits of technological progress cannot be easily separated from the evils of capital accumulation. In transferring production of industrial goods to the South, the North has created a new monster, a Promethean Frankenstein which it may not be able to control. The Northerners still want to consume energy and goods at a great rate; they may even appreciate the fact that the "dirty" production processes will take place on another continent. The industrial boom in the Third World and the increased use and aspirations for motor vehicles are leading the people of the South into higher consumption of energy with no corresponding means to control pollution.

We have already mentioned that the North has elevated its standard of living to the obscene level of enjoying average incomes that are nearly 24 times higher than those in the South. This difference in consumption is far greater, however, if we look at how much energy is used per inhabitant of each area; for some countries the comparison is extreme, even ridiculous:

1986 Energy Use

The average U.S. citizen consumed 50,000 times as many BTUs of energy as the average citizen of Honduras.

We may be sure that in backward Honduras, and especially in industrializing countries like Brazil, Malaysia, and Indonesia, the pressures of capitalist development on both producers and consumers will mean that energy use increases many times over without ever reaching the standard of living of the North. And why should the North expect that the South can control the effects of its energy consumption, when the rich countries have performed so poorly themselves?

NO MORE DOOM AND GLOOM

Where can capitalism go from here, now that it seems to have conquered the world only to end up destroying it?

The primary purpose of this book has been to unveil economic realities and deflate the myths of progress which characterize the capitalist world system and its vision of itself. The 20th century version of these myths would encourage us to believe that, just as the world is about to choke to death, "technology" will come to the rescue. Perhaps technology will be necessary for the resuscitation of the world's ecology and economy, but it will require some system that is more democratic and more socially responsible than market capitalism to control its use.

There are signs, although sometimes vague or timid ones, that humankind has the ability and the generosity to restructure global society in a way that dignifies human life and protects all planetary life. Even as the dust is settling from the demise of the so-called "socialist empire" in the Soviet Union, we ought to take notice that social democratic and democratic socialist political parties still exist all over the world. For years they have been caught in a difficult dilemma that curtailed the development of real alternatives. To their credit, these parties have always disclaimed connection to Stalinism and authoritarian state systems erected and labeled in honor of "Socialism" or its mythical offspring, "Communism". On the other hand, social democrats often served as the liberal handmaidens of capitalist development, thinking that they were engaging in progressive planning and management toward "social" ends, only to find that they had often better served the requirements of capital itself.

Still, in an imperfect world, it is in the advanced capitalist countries with strong social democratic parties and a history of dedication to the rights of workers that high levels of social well-being and freedom have been achieved for large majorities of the people. A small country like Sweden has developed a welfare state which protects almost everyone while also cooperating with its industrial sector, which is still capitalist, to produce one of the world's highest standards of living. Other large countries like Germany, France, and Italy (and to a lesser extent, Japan) have not enjoyed the benefits of having socialist parties in power for long periods of time. Nevertheless, because of continuous pressure from the Left, they have instituted egalitarian policies - in favor of such things as universal health care, paid leave from work for mothers, day care for children, workers' rights to benefits and retraining - which have created a sense of social well-being, thereby avoiding the kind of serious division between rich and poor which exists in the United States.

Sweden has also embarked upon a program of environmental safety within the workplace and throughout the society that is enviable. The workers' committees in factories have the right to shut down production if they feel there are hazardous conditions on the shop floor. Voters decided to simply eliminate the nuclear power industry because Swedish scientists, like those in every other country, have no way to guarantee the safe disposal of nuclear waste over a period of ten thousand years or more. While Sweden may not be a model which other European countries can copy, at least it can act as a signpost. One of the most significant sentiments to grow there, one not to the liking of Sweden's industrialists, is the idea that the economy does not have to expand, that the present standard of living is more than adequate for all. This is a novel idea for the countries of the North: technological advances, conservation of energy, and recycling of waste might allow a modern industrial society to consume less rather than more. If the mature capitalist countries begin to curb the voracious appetites that have led them to devour the earth, will they still be capitalist?

"WAIT A MINUTE!"

You can almost hear five billion people in the rest of the world beginning to yell in protest, saying:

The world does not resemble Sweden.

Why indulge in unnecessary dreaming about the world approaching the standards of the most favored nations of the North?

Let's look, then, at one of the poorest parts of the South, a tiny part of India that has almost four times as many people as Sweden:

Much of the world does resemble Kerala.

Kerala is a southwestern coastal region that is more crowded and even poorer than the rest of India. It has 27 million people crammed onto land that once served as a productive and super-exploitative plantation area for the British Empire. In spite of its extreme poverty, Kerala has stressed radical equality for the past 40 years and thereby achieved certain living conditions for its people that are remarkable. In their book, *Kerala: Radical Reform as Development in an Indian State*, Richard Franke and Barbara Chasin have revealed that Kerala displays quality of life indicators that are closer to First World levels than Third World ones:

Quality of Life in Kerala - 1986

	Kerala	India	Other Low Income Countries
Per Capita GNP	$182	$290	$200
Adult Literacy	78%	43%	48%
Life Expectancy	68	57	52
Infant Mortality	22	86	106
Birth Rate	22	32	43

(Infant Mortality and Birth Rates are per thousand inhabitants)

In Kerala, a coalition called the Left Democratic Front has offered basic programs that are carried out with the democratic involvement of most of the population:

1. Land has been purchased from landlords and redistributed to individual peasant owners.

2. Health care for all, health care training, and public sanitation have been a top priority.

3. Education opportunity, particularly for women, is highly emphasized.

4. Basic food availability is guaranteed through government licensed shops, school lunch programs, and feeding programs for mothers and infants.

The State of Kerala is too poor to be Nirvana and too closely tied into the overall capitalist economy of India to embark on its own democratic socialist path of economic development. Kerala's own remaining capitalists and landlords are likely to invest their money in neighboring states where labor is cheaper; likewise, big-time Indian capitalists are wary of setting up industrial plants in Kerala, where labor unions are strong and demand better treatment than elsewhere. Still Kerala offers a remarkably dignified and healthy life to its inhabitants in spite of its extreme poverty and its isolation from investment and "growth." If there were a world economic system which rewarded a combination of grassroots democracy and the very efficient use of very limited public resources, then foreign capital would surely be invested in creating a productive base for a higher standard of living in Kerala.

Kerala offers a very attractive model to other Third World countries, but with one caveat: for a variety of complex reasons having to do with Indian politics and the fact that India is a huge country, Kerala has not been crushed by other pro-capitalist factions or regions. Elsewhere in the world, especially in the Western Hemisphere, those who have wanted the "freedom to invest" in the exploitation of labor have always been able to muster military force and political terror, from both domestic and foreign sources, to wipe out straightforward systems of redistribution such as that practiced in Kerala.

We have only invoked the names of Kerala and Sweden to remind the reader of the following: that precisely in the heyday of the industrial revolution in Europe widespread opposition among ordinary people created an anti-capitalist force and rationale which exists to this day; even in the far reaches of the British Empire workers movements were disseminating socialist literature and forming peasant leagues that formed the basis of today's Democratic Front in Kerala.

The history of democratic and working class movements tells us that people can change the course of capitalist development and even curtail its worst excesses. Sweden was still a backward country in the throes of early industrialization when its socialist parties began pressuring for social change. In fact, at the end of the nineteenth century throughout Europe and the United States, there was a vast array of leftist opposition to the systemic problems induced by capitalist development. We are now witnessing the same kind of struggle in the rest of the world, caught up in its own process of industrialization, as people attempt to assess the social claims of the wage earners against the privileges of an international capitalist class.

Kerala, at the opposite extreme of the earth and far from the resources available for a comfortable earthly existence in Sweden, has shown that democratic left movements, even under the constraints of a larger capitalist economy, can offer remarkable changes in the quality of life. However, being a citizen of Sweden and a citizen of Kerala are extremely different propositions. It is obvious that the billions of earth dwellers in the South are at a terrible disadvantage compared to the old proletariat of the North, because the new proletarians are so distant from the sources of wealth and power. Furthermore, the earth has announced that it is no longer willing to be used and abused in the fashion which has enriched the North and impoverished the South.

ECOLOGICAL LIMITS TO FURTHER CAPITALIST GROWTH

We are realizing that after 500 years on its present course the further development of capitalism faces two major and nearly insurmountable ecological obstacles. One, given the way energy and raw materials are consumed today, the world cannot support the opulent standard of living of the North, let alone grant that life style to the majority of people who live elsewhere. Two, it will utterly destroy the liveability of the globe if we continue to behave as if such consumption will be possible in the future.

The earth and its people need to make enormous changes in their relationship. It is not at all likely that left-leaning political parties, labor unions, and religious humanitarians of the North could, through moral persuasion alone, force their advanced nations to change their ways; that is, the rich nations are not likely to adopt a monumental program of charity directed toward the majority of wage laborers around the world. Even the working classes of the North are rich compared to their potential "compañeros" in the South, and not likely, out of pure altruism, to sacrifice some of that status in order to benefit those who live thousands of miles away. And perhaps that is as it should be.

We must recognize that the distance most people put between themselves and the social disasters of the world is "normal," not excusable by any means, but the same reaction displayed ever since the European conquest began. The cynicism of the rich veils their complicity in the profit-taking on the other side of the world; the ignorance of the majority is compounded by their lack of political power, especially pertaining to things that occur in the international political economy. At various times in the 19th and 20th centuries the material self-interest of many Northern workers was furthered by imperialism; today they are not likely to oppose the oppression of other peoples unless they are convinced that there are important considerations of both self-interest and solidarity, so that they cease to trust the compulsive capitalist pattern of ever greater consumption.

What about "The Destruction of the Earth?" Could this very real threat be appreciated by most people in the North? Could it seize the attention of people of various social classes, too?

Ecological consciousness in today's world is a survival mechanism - not as pretty a notion as charity or the grace of self-sacrifice - but a very compelling idea if it can be connected to a feeling of responsibility for the global human community. Survival is a selfish concept or, at the least, self-interested. If environmentalism can become a widespread notion of universal survival, perhaps the Northerners can be compelled to act in the interests of the whole world.

Is the global picture too big to comprehend? Could the rich countries revive the notion of social democracy, maybe even strive toward democratic socialism, because they finally notice that they must be engaged in everyday struggles to save their earth? The promising aspect of environmental solidarity is that it could give concrete expression to the dream of global cooperation that social reformers and revolutionaries have always hoped was just over the horizon.

Chapter 23

RED AND GREEN

"There is something important about women in Guatemala, especially Indian women, and that something is her relationship with the earth-between the earth and the mother. The earth gives food and the mother gives life.... this feeling is born in women because of the responsibilities they have, which men do not have."

- Rigoberta Menchu

"It is a radical proposal: teachers, workers, doctors, artists, men and women in the countryside, writers, rubber tree tappers, journalists, fishermen, small businessmen, engineers, and all other people who, like those above, construct the present with their work. For them we must build the future."

- Lula (Luis da Silva)

RED AND GREEN

One of the signs that there is the possibility of changing the world is that the people of the North find themselves listening to the voices of the South. The clearest expressions of solidarity with the earth and all its people come from those who are organizing at the most basic level. Rigoberta Menchu - revolutionary, Christian catechist, and spokeswoman for the Indians of Guatemala- reminds us that the earth and women share a special relationship in preserving and promoting life. And Lula, the metal worker who may one day be elected President of Brazil, is among those who insist on a definition of work which goes beyond traditional conceptions of a certain segment of the industrial working class and includes all who support themselves by their own labor.

When so many in the North are focusing on themselves or on very limited and fragmented notions of liberation, those in the South are often quicker to recognize the global nature of our predicament. If our long era of rapacious capitalism is to be overcome, it will be through alliances forged across classes and across continents, between the earth and its human inhabitants, and between people who work with their hands and those who work with their minds.

Is there a scenario for containing or surpassing capitalism? It seems doubtful that there will be a socialist society suddenly created by the simultaneous uprising of heroic and well-intentioned people from all over the world. Perhaps, if humankind is lucky, we will see some process of revolutionary reformism; that is, reformism that means something more than little adjustments of the wheels that drive capitalism and instead leads toward a steady evolution of social, economic, cultural, and political structures that can harness or replace the old capitalist forms.

The spectre of environmental collapse is more frightening to some members of the capitalist class than the ghost of communism returned. If environmentalism represents the means by which working people can establish bonds of solidarity across the continents, it can also offer a way to break down the narrow upper class loyalties among the international bourgeoisie. Moreover, ecological consciousness has the potential to dissolve that paralyzing separation of human energy that has characterized industrial capitalism and bolstered its authority: the distinction made between the interests and desires of the mental workers and the manual workers.

At this point it would be nice to have Marx available to write a manifesto for us, except that if we really hope to enjoy a red and green future, maybe we need something that stops short of the near-utopianism of Marx and avoids the Eurocentric pride that has plagued both capitalism and socialism since their conception. If we look back to the time of the original Communist Manifesto, we find the prophetic words that are now also so discomforting:

> *"The bourgeois period of history has to create the material basis of the new world — on the one hand the universal intercourse that is founded upon the mutual dependency of mankind, and the means of that intercourse; on the other the development of the productive power of man and the transformation of material production into scientific domination of natural agencies... When a great social revolution shall have mastered the results of the bourgeois epoch, the market of the world and the modern powers of production, and subjected them to the common control of the most advanced people, then only will human progress cease to resemble that hideous pagan idol, who would not drink the nectar but from the skulls of the slain."*
> -Karl Marx, "The Future Results of British Rule in India" - 1853

Perhaps we have finally reached that moment in history when the "bourgeois" have done all they can to "create the material basis for the new world" in a more fully developed "world market," but it is difficult to share Marx's faith, which he caught from his European bourgeois contemporaries, in either the "scientific domination of natural agencies" or in the "control of the most advanced people." In fact, a red and green future that promotes world equality and world ecology will have to feature something different: the scientific co-operation with natural agencies on the one hand, and the shared control of the least advanced people; to that we might add, "the productive power of man" must be balanced by the productive and reproductive power of woman, including her instincts for peaceful organization and survival.

A RED AND GREEN POLITICAL ECONOMY

Our task is to create a new world system that can preserve the Earth while furthering the opportunities for all humans to enjoy freedom, dignity, and equality in their daily lives. Since we lack a manifesto and an idealized program for this new democratic socialist future, let us offer instead some practical notions of the antidote to the capitalist mania:

1. There are Social Democratic parties in the North - which in their broad range include the French Socialist Party, the German Social Democrats, the Democratic Party of the Left (the former Communist Party) and the Socialist Party in Italy, the Socialist and Communist Parties of Japan, the Labor Party of Great Britain. These parties (in conjunction with smaller groupings of the radical left, the environmentalist Greens, and the radical republican parties) have a chance to assume power simultaneously in 5 of the 6 largest capitalist economies of the world, which happen to be the healthier part of the dominant North (with the U.S., the single greatest national economy and the society most lacking in democratic socialist influence, on the decline.)

2. There are emerging Democratic Socialist parties in the South - such as the Workers Party of Brazil, the Mexican Democratic Revolutionary Party, the African National Congress in South Africa, the lively democratic workers movement in Korea - that may have the chance to assume or share power in their respective countries. Aided by progressive movements emerging among different religious and cultural groups, these democratic socialist movements could start linking their policies and economies to the social democratic tendencies of the North. (In addition there are the three gigantic countries of the earth - China, India, and Russia - could they, with some encouragement from a changing world economy, have the potential of moving toward democratic development, too?)

3. In the future, the North must stop becoming richer. Since its present level of consumption is already more than sufficient to sustain all its people in a high degree of comfort, the North must start gathering its surpluses and transferring them towards the development of the South.

4. The limits on consumption in the North will not mean an end to productive and scientific advances that benefit the Northerners themselves. Investment of part of the economic surplus must be devoted to new technologies which reduce the per capita use of energy, the health dangers in the workplace and the environment, and the amount of waste and pollution of all kinds.

5. A very large portion of the capital surplus of the North - trillions of dollars annually - must be invested in the rest of the world; this wealth will be transferred to the South, not as charity but as investment in such things as:

- supporting industrialization with only the most ecologically correct fuels and products

- supporting the democratic socialist governments which promote small scale, non-exploitative agriculture

- paying rent to maintain the rain forests at their present size while allowing for limited and friendly habitation

- investing in a social infrastructure of healthcare, public sanitation, education, and mass transportation

6. The North will provide management through private and public agencies in order to insure the sound investment of its trillions of dollars. Industrial and agricultural investment in the South will be required to produce a business-like surplus in order to indicate productivity. However, the returns on investment from ecologically sound industrialization will remain in the South and will go towards reinvestment and higher wages for labor.

7. A final trade-off will be made between North and South in regard to military armaments: in return for large amounts of investment, the nations of the South will be required to reduce their armed forces drastically and forego the purchase or production of military hardware. The same restriction will apply to the North.

Why should such a plan for equalizing the status and rights of North and South be attractive to the average citizens of the North? First of all, there is a growing consciousness among many people in the North that environmental concerns and efforts for discouraging warfare must be dealt with on a global level. Beyond this, a new era of global equity will promote the long-term welfare of Northern workers. There will be no reason for Northern workers to lose jobs through the transferral of production facilities to areas which promise the highest possible exploitation of labor. The stringent changes towards environmentally sound production in the North and the production of new tools and technologies for the South will require the skilled labor of the North and will emphasize the importance of this labor input over the need for cheap energy. An immense boom in production and services will occur, as new technologies vie to replace the fossil-fueled-industrial revolution of the past with a renewable energy revolution of the future. Countless products need to be invented, redesigned, and perfected.

If the nations of the North do not pursue a new course, then their only alternative is to keep following the course which sanctifies the "free market" and condones the means used to keep the rest of the world subservient to the advanced capitalist nations. That is, the North would be tempted to institute even more vicious versions of its current practices: increasing "austerity" under the control of organizations like the International Monetary Fund; continuing reliance on fascist local governments to control their restive populations; new reliance on religious systems that teach obedience to authority and reverence for capital; and the re-emergence of racist doctrines that defend the dehumanization of the non-white populations of the earth. Will the citizens of the North, presuming they still have democratic governments that entitle them to pursue their own destinies, be willing to keep imposing such a regime upon the South?

IN CONCLUSION

The foregoing list of economic alternatives is not meant to suggest only the things which the North must do for the South. It is presumed that the South will make important, maybe the most important, contributions to a new world system - social inventions in terms of political participation and racial harmony; new kinds of compatibility between religious and secular philosophies; more reasonable technologies for using the earth's resources. On the other hand, the above prescriptions reflect a certain kind of reality: the North controls the vast majority of wealth and military force on the Earth. Even if social democratic representatives from the North try to avoid gestures of cultural imperialism, their managerial power and technological edge will undoubtedly cause friction with the democratic socialist forces that emerge in the South.

If democratic socialism is to eventually exercise some control over the world system created by capitalism, it will only be by a painful process which somehow deals with the whole economic network. Recent history has shown us that there is no opportunity to resign from a world created by the capitalist conquistadors, there is no isolated and bucolic existence possible for fledgling developing countries, and so, in a sense, only partial self-determination is possible for the nations of the South. That is to say, the kind of international thinking that is necessary to overcome this dangerous end stage of capitalism will undoubtedly bring some restrictions with it. On the one hand, we must hope that by controlling the capitalist consumer culture that we can allow regional cultures to assert themselves and flourish throughout the world. On the

other hand, the measures that will be necessary to control and eliminate militarism and weapons production on all continents will require the strictest adherence to international norms, whether through the United Nations or some new body.

The emphasis on themes of economic, religious, and political conquest by a European system dominated by a capitalist class points to one of the woeful inadequacies of this book: there is no room to recount the richness of non-European cultures nor to give any adequate account of the continuous resistance of various peoples and social classes to the systemic forms of oppression and exploitation. There is no intention to discount the value of such popular struggles, nor to deny the fact that any anti-capitalist critique relies upon the ability of common people to identify the causes of their oppression. People throughout the Americas, industrial workers in Korea, peasants in the Philippines, miners in South Africa, and women in almost every nation are continuously engaged in the dangerous effort of asserting their rights against the claims of capital.

The people of the South have labored constantly for centuries to build the New World and enrich the Old; they know a patience and self-discipline which are beyond the comprehension of most people in the North, but they have no desire to be the ones who support the new colossus of transnational production.

The people of the North must remember that their traditions of equality and freedom also originated in the long struggles of common people to limit arbitrary power and safeguard the general welfare. If they can identify with the common destiny of the people in the South, resist the temptations of racism and consumerism, and reinvigorate their own traditions of democratic socialism, then there is some hope for the world.

The kinds of economic and political arrangements with which the North must comply constitute neither charity to the poor nor unfair impositions upon the rich; they constitute movement toward shared economic control and responsible democratic rule of a revised world system. There are, of course, serious doubts about the abilities of the social democratic parties which inhabit the North to pursue such a program; perhaps their democratic and socialist sensibilities are not sufficiently strong to overcome their habitual deference to capital and nationalism. Existing socialist and left parties are in need of a red and green revival: the growing green awareness must overcome the petty concerns of comfortable Northern bureaucrats; the red example of the new people's movements in the South must energize the old blood of democratic socialism that once prospered in Europe.

Perhaps such a future seems unlikely at a time when the leaders of the capitalist system are proclaiming the "New World Order" and celebrating the conquest of the Northern war machine over their ex-client in the Middle East. We might remember that 500 years ago the chances of remaking the world seemed dim. Yet, a lonely and acquisitive Columbus, driven by courage and hard-hearted faith and an image of a smaller world, brought Europe to the Americas. Columbus' contemporaries did not lack knowledge - many of them understood the general geography of the world better than he did - but they did not dare take the risk of proving their hypotheses by sailing West.

Today many people around the world understand that the engines of capital and consumption that drive the world system have only operated for the benefit of a few people in a few countries. They also know that the material means for building a just world are at hand. What seems to be lacking, especially in the North, is a more generous appreciation of the spirit and attributes of humanity.

Where would Columbus be if he arrived on the scene today? Would he still be sailing westward on a lonely route toward fantasies of wealth, beset by conflicting emotions of egotism and religious passion?

Or would Columbus be a humble man or woman of the Americas, sailing Eastward toward Europe, more than willing to share the bounty of the earth with his or her neighbors in the North? Perhaps our modern day Columbus would discover that the seeds of liberty and equality could still be planted and, with some intensive cultivation, could prosper throughout the whole world.

NOTES

Chapter 1, COLUMBUS AND THE CAPITALIST CONQUEST, 1492-1992 (pages 1-5)

*"One who has gold...": Michel Beaud, *A History of Capitalism, 1500-1980*. New York: Monthly Review Press, 1983, p.19. *"Let us in the name...": Howard Zinn, *A People's History of the United States*. New York: Harper and Row, 1980, p.4. *"On my arrival...": Charles Duff, *The Truth About Columbus*. New York: Random House, 1936, p. 151. *"The Indians..." and "hands chopped off": Gianni Granzotto, *Christopher Columbus*, New York: Doubleday, 1985, p. 162 and p. 223. Some other books about Columbus: Samuel Eliot Morison, *Admiral of the Ocean Sea*, Boston: Little, Brown, 1942 and *Christopher Columbus: Mariner*, Boston: Little, Brown, 1955; Hans Koning, *Columbus: His Enterprise*, New York: Monthly Review Press, 1976; Kirkpatrick Sale, *The Conquest of Paradise*, New York: Knopf, 1990. Granzotto's book is rather positive toward Columbus, though capable of rendering straightforward criticism; Sale's work is more negative, while offering many illuminating details of Columbus' life and times; his environmental critique is congenial with many of the arguments of this book. *Karl Marx: *Capital*, Vols. I, II, and III, New York: International Publishers, 1967. The reader will find several quotes from Marx in this book, which should suggest that this critique is linked to the 150 year old tradition of trying to understand and change capitalist society which is known as "Marxism." This does not mean that the author "believes" in Marxism, accepts everything Marx wrote or predicted, or is interested in the development of a strict form of Marxist logic. The Marxist tradition, in its undogmatic sense (for example, see the articles and books associated with the *Monthly Review*), is still well-suited to investigating economic and political life and understanding how the world works; it also carries with it the commitment of Marx and Engels and other early socialists: to engage in the practical advocacy of the rights and freedoms of working people - that is, on behalf of the overwhelming majority of the world's inhabitants, those who actually produce the food and objects, the machinery and services, the art and ideas that make our existence both possible and enjoyable. *"Thus the eternal God...": Zinn, *A People's History...*, p. 3.

Chapter 2, ENTREPRENEUR SHIP (pages 6-9)

*Percentages of the profit: Granzotto, *Christopher Columbus*. *"they are a very loving race...": Duff, *The Truth About Columbus*, p. 130-131. *"We Spanish suffer ..": Beaud, *A History of Capitalism*, p. 18. *"It was his voyage to Guinea...": Granzotto, p. 46-47. *Columbus cheating Rodrigo Triano: Granzotto, p.139. *Columbus and Pinzon: Granzotto. *Columbus and sainthood: Granzotto, p.281

Chapter 3, HARD-HEARTED BUSINESS- HARD-HEARTED FAITH (pages 10-13)

*Columbus sells Indians as slaves, then begins to massacre them in Hispaniola: Granzotto, p. 222. *The original population of Hispaniola, 200,000 to 300,000: this figure is on the conservative side and comes from Eric Williams, *The History of the Caribbean: From Columbus to Castro*, New York: Harper and Row, 1971, p. 33. The numbers vary wildly for estimating the population of the native civilizations in the New World. One of the wilder numbers: Kirkpatrick Sale, in *The Conquest of Paradise*, uses a number of 8 million for the island of Hispaniola by making use of a rather questionable academic projection of Columbus' own estimates. See the footnote below on the original population of America. *Burning Indians at the stake: Eduardo Galeano, *Genesis* (volume I of *Memories of Fire*, New York: Pantheon, 1987, p. 51. *"God almighty..." and "That which is common...": Galeano, p.221. *"Sometimes the Scripture...": Charles M. Segal, David C. Steinbeck, *Puritans, Indians, and Manifest Destiny*, New York: Putnam, 1977. *Franklin: "If it be the design...": *200 Years in Cumberland County*, Carlisle, PA: Hamilton Library and Cumberland County Historical Society, 1951. *"I went down on my knees...": Zinn, *A People's History...*, p. 305. *"So savage..." and "Are there Christians...": Galeano, *Genesis*, p. 57; Oviedo, or Gonzalo Fernandez de Oviedo y Valdes, wrote an elaborate *Historia General y Natural de las Indias*. *Original Indian Population of Latin America and the Caribbean: Russell Thorton, *American Indian Holocaust and Survival*, Norman: University of Oklahoma Press, 1987. Of all the attempts to estimate the populations of the original inhabitants of the Americas, Thorton's seems most reasonable. He suggests that early researchers (like James Mooney of the Smithsonian, 1928) downplayed the numbers because they did not want to discuss the magnitude of the slaughter or because they did not have the analytic tools to project backwards from the very scarce populations in North America around 1900. On the other hand, some more recent writers may have been tempted to overestimate the original Indian population unnecessarily because of their sympathy with the Indians' plight and their way of life. Thorton puts his numbers at 7 million for North America and 65 million for the rest of the Hemisphere, between the estimates of Dobyns - 112.5 million native Americans in 1492 - and Denevan - 57.3 million. (W.M. Denevan, *The Native Population of the Americas in 1492*, Madison: University of Wisconsin Press, 1976; Henry Dobyns, *Native American Historical Demography*, University of Indiana Press, 1976.) Another interesting population estimate comes from Thorton: the number of American buffalo or bison- 60,000,000 in 1492; 20,000,000 in 1850; less than 1000 in 1895. *Santo Domingo: Galeano, *Genesis*, p. 72. *"What was new.." and "From its first...": Beaud, *A History of Capitalism*, pp. 23 and p. 42.

Chapter 4, MOUNTAINS OF SILVER AND GOLD (pages 14-17)

*population and wealth of Potosi: Eduardo Galeano, *The Open Veins of Latin America*, New York: Monthly Review, 1973, p.31. *Story of the Indian miners and the quotation "I don't want to see this portrait of Hell...": Galeano, *Genesis*, p. 172. *non-working Spaniards: 17th century *Treatise on Necessary Policy*, by Don Martin Gonzales de Cellorigo, cited in Galeano, *Genesis*, p. 174 *"We discovered the realms...": Galeano, *Genesis*, p. 160. *The richest mine: Galeano, *Open Veins*, p. 47. *16,000,000 kilograms of silver: Galeano, *Open Veins*, p. 33. *"There is no people..": Galeano, *Genesis*, p.248. *"they are all lazy...": Galeano, *Open Veins*, p. 53. *Sepulveda: Galeano, *Genesis*, p.123. *Bartholeme de las Casas: Lewis Hanke, *Bartolome del las Casas*, Philadelphia: University of Pennsylvania, 1952 and

Juan Friede, *Bartolome de las Casas Precursor del Anticolonialismo*, Mexico: Siglo XXI, 1976. *"left no other nexus...": Karl Marx, *The Communist Manifesto*.

Chapter 5, SLAVERY: THE WEALTH OF EUROPE (pages 18-21)

*Ferdnand Braudel, *Civilization and Capitalism, vol. II, The Wheels of Commerce*, New York: Harper and Row, 1986. pp. 272-273. *gradations of color: Carter Godwin Woodson, *The Negro in Our History*, Washington: Associated Publishers, 1922. *Historian Giao Prado: cited in Galeano, *Open Veins*, p. 92. *Ferdnand Braudel, *Civilization and Capitalism, Vol. III, The Perspective of the World*, New York: Harper and Row, 1984. p. 440. *Basil Davidson, *The African Slave Trade*, Boston: Little, Brown, 1961. *lower estimates of slaves arrived in New World: Philip Curtin, *The African Slave Trade: A Census*, Madison, Unversity of Wisconsin Press, 1969. *Barbados: Eric Williams, *History of the Caribbean*, p. 136. *imports to England: Williams, p. 151. *slaves in Jamaica and mortality: Williams, p. 146. *"The profits of the sugar...": Adam Smith, *The Wealth of Nations*. *Davenant quote: Williams, p. 143. *"was a magnificent superstructure...": Williams, p. 153. *"There is nothing...": Williams, p. 136. *du Tertre: Williams p. 204. *Quakers in Barbados: Williams, p. 186.

Chapter 6, WHO OPPOSED GENOCIDE IN THE NEW WORLD? (pages 22-25)

*Population estimates come from Thorton, *American Indian Holocaust and Survival*. The estimates for Europe do not include the population of European Russia. *"Turn Jesus Christ into...": Hanke, *Bartolome de las Casas*. *Friar Montesinos: Galeano, *Genesis*, 57. *"to go to hell...": Galeano, p. 84. *Las Casas, his own book, *A Very Brief Account of the Destruction of the Indies*. Las Casas, paradoxically, was a man who loved Christopher Columbus and was responsible for transcribing all his notebooks. Edmundo O'Gorman, in *The Invention of America*, Bloomington: University of Indiana Press, 1961, p. 19, points out that "Las Casas' fundamental premise is the providential concept of history" and then he quotes Las Casas to demonstrate his view of Columbus' role in history: "the discovery of America appears as the fulfillment of a divine plan carried out by a man chosen for the purpose." *Hakluyt: Williams, p. 76. *"Under the priest's tutorship...": Galeano, *Genesis*, p. 227. *"The Jesuits had taught...": Galeano, *Faces and Masks*, p. 34. *two Italian priests: Philip Caraman, *The Lost Paradise*, New York: Seabury, 1976, p. 108. *two million Indian slaves: Caraman, p. 58. *"The Society of Jesus may pride itself...": Caraman p. 300. *Priests as revolutionaries: W.H. Timmons, *Morelos of Mexico*, El Paso: Texas Western University Press, 1963; Ubaldo Vargas Martinez, *Morelos: Siervo de la Nacion*, Mexico City: Porrua, 1966. *Morelos, driver of oxen - Timmons, p. 7.

PART II - THE CAPITALIST CONQUEST OF CENTRAL AMERICA (page 27)

*Korean maquiladoras in Guatemala: medium size factories for the assembly of such things as textiles and electronics are flourishing, particularly around the small city of Chimaltenango, an hour west of Guatemala City - information gathered by author on visit to Guatemala in 1990.

Chapter 7, WHAT IF THEY STOPPED BRINGING YOUR CUP OF COFFEE IN THE MORNING? pages 28-31)

*"Communist support of the poor" (another neo-fascist slogan was "Be a Patriot, Kill a Priest!"): Tom Barry, Deb Preusch, *Central American Fact Book*, New York: Grove Press, 1986, p. 201. *"The cause of our problems...": Tom Barry, *Roots of Rebellion: Land and Hunger in Central America*, Boston: South End Press, 1987. The works of Tom Barry, Deb Preusch, and the Resource Center in Albuquerque, New Mexico, are indispensible for an understanding of Central America and Mexico and their relationships with the United States. *"unconventional warfare": news report on "All Things Considered," National Public Radio, April 25, 1990. *95% of exports: Barry, *Roots of Rebellion*, p. 26. *"Men were taken in big batches": Thomas P. Anderson, *Matanza*, Lincoln: University of Nebraska, 1971, quoted in Barry, *Roots of Rebellion*, p.26. *coffee and poverty statistics: ibid., pp. 16 and 24. *Landowning families % of ownership: ibid., p. 51. *"the oligarch you see..": ibid., p. 44. *D'Aubuisson behind assassination of Archbishop Romero: Barry and Preusch, *Central American Fact Book*, p. 205. The former head of Salvadorean Central Intelligence directly implicated D'Aubuisson in the killing in 1985. *"pathological killer": ibid., p. 206. *"You Germans were very intelligent...": Alexander Cockburn, "Beat the Devil," *The Nation*, May 15, 1989.

Chapter 8, ONE RED BANANA CAN SPOIL THE BUNCH (pages 32-36)

*Among a number of good sources on Guatemala: Jim Handy, *Gift of the Devil: A History of Guatemala*, Boston: South End Press, 1984; *Guatemala in Rebellion: Unfinished History*, ed. by Jonathan L. Fried, Marvin E. Gettleman, Deborah T. Levenson, and Nancy Peckenham. New York: Grove Press, 1983; Tom Barry, *Guatemala: A Country Guide*, Albuquerque: The Interhemispheric Education Resource Center, 1989. *United Fruit... 3,000,000 acres: Max Gordon, "A Case History of U.S. Subversion in Guatemala," *Guatemala in Rebellion*, p. 55 and 56. The information on the direct business ties of the Eisenhower government to the United Fruit Company are elaborated, with many more supporting characters than named here, in the books listed above. The 1953 coup was a public relations masterpiece for the United States and the Fruit Company, because the U.S. public had no idea about the realities of Guatemala and was fed a steady stream of half truths and lies by the CIA and the United Fruit publicity department, which could plant stories in the North American press at will. Edward L. Bernays, public relations consultant for the United Fruit Company at the time, once wrote the following revealing description of his kind of work: "the conscious and intelligent manipulation of the organized habits of the masses is an important element in democratic society. Those who manipulate this unseen mechanism of society constitute an invisible government which is the true ruling power of our country... It is the intelligent minorities which need to make use of propaganda continuously and systematically. In the active proselytizing of minorities in whom selfish interests and public interests coincide lie the progress and development of America." (quoted on p. 59, Jonas and Tobias, *Guatemala*, Berkeley: NACLA, 1974.) *one half of all workers organized...1,500,000 acres of land redistributed: *Guatemala in Rebellion*, pp. 53 and 62. *Arbenz's land: ibid. p. 52. *86% in poverty in 1989 according to a University of San Carlos study: Tom Barry, *Guatemala: A Country Guide*, p. 5. *disappeared labor leaders: Robert Morris, "Coke Adds Life?", *Guatemala in Rebellion*, p. 176. *religious workers killed or forced to flee, churches closed: "A Priest Among the People: An Interview with Father Celso," *Guatemala in Rebellion*, p. 224. *forced labor for Indians: Alain Y. Dessant, "Land and Labor after Independence," *Guatemala in Rebellion*, p. 27. *"Who taught these wretches...": Father Celso, p. 225-6. *"the acquisition...": Handy, *Gift of the Devil*, p. 253. *"not even the lives...": Handy, p. 255. *Cerezo, "30% of the power": *Guatemala Elections 1986*, Guatemala City: Inforpress, 1987. *Investment in radio stations: Susan D. Rose and Quentin Schultz, in their study of Guatemalan evangelicalism for the American Academy of Arts and Sciences, "The Fundamentalism Project," which is scheduled to be published in late 1992 as "The Evangelical Awakening in Guatemala: Fundamentalist Impact on Education and Media," Chapter 15 of *Fundamentalisms and Society: Reclaiming the Sciences, the Family, and Education*, Chicago: University of Chicago Press. *U.S. businessmen, "Shoot him or...": Allan Nairn, "To Defend Our Way of Life: Interview with a U.S. Businessman," *Guatemala in Rebellion*, p. 89.

Chapter 9, NICARAGUA: TRYING TO ESCAPE THE GRINGO (pages 37-40)

*William Walker and Cornelius Vanderbilt: William D. Scroggs, *Filibusters and Financiers*, New York: MacMillan, 1916. *quotes from *Harper's Weekly* and *The Richmond Inquirer*: cited by George Black, *Good Neighbors*, New York, Pantheon, 1989, pp.6-7. *"the conservatism of slavery..." and "with the negro slave...": William Walker, *The War in Nicaragua*, Mobile: S.H. Goetzel, 1860, p. 259 and p. 261. Walker went to a great deal of trouble to outline his goals in this book written after his ouster from Central America; although he had earned the enmity of Vanderbilt, he was perspicacious enough to know that arguments for slavery had to be aimed at those who controlled the capital in the U.S. and backed up by religious rationale: "'by the Cross you shalt conquer' as is clearly written in the pages of history." p. 430. *Vanderbilt, Walker, and the Transit Co.: the intrigues over control of the route to California are nicely described by Scroggs in *Filibusters and Financiers*. *Somoza, "You tell me tomorrow...": Allan Nairn, in "Defend our way of life...", *Guatemala in Rebellion*, p. 92. *meat consumption: Tom Barry, *Roots of Rebellion*, p. 35. *development of liberation theology within Nicaragua: Roger Lancaster, *Thanks to God and the Revolution: Popular Religion and Class Consciousness in the New Nicaragua*, New York: Columbia University Press, 1988; and Penny Lernoux, *People of God*, New York: Viking, 1989. Conor Cruise O'Brien, "God and Man in Nicaragua," *The Atlantic Monthly*, August 1986. *Somoza owned 20% of farmland: Barry, *Roots*, p. 132. *good discussion of the problems and reconciliation between the Sandinistas and the Miskitos in Lernoux's *People of God*.

Chapter 10, LIBERATION FROM THE STRUCTURES OF POVERTY AND OPPRESSION (pages 41-44)

*300,000 base communities: Lernoux, *People of God*, p. 409. *"They say we are Marxists...": Roger N. Lancaster, *Thanks to God and the Revolution*, p. 85. *other good sources on liberation theology: Philip Berryman, *the

Religious Roots of Rebellion, Maryknoll: Orbis, 1984 (and a number of other books published by this press run by the Maryknoll Catholic order which is very active in Central America); Penny Lernoux, *Cry of the People*, New York: Penguin, 1982; Gustavo Gutierrez, *A Theology of Liberation* (1973) and *The Power of the Poor in History* (1983), Maryknoll, NY: Orbis. *"is not set up to seek earthly glory...": Lernoux, *People of God*, p. 22. *"the basis for...": ibid. p. 93. *"sin of institutionalized violence": ibid. p. 25. *850 priests and nuns martyred: ibid. p. 95. *Solentiname: see Ernesto Cardinal, *The Gospel of Solentiname*, Maryknoll, NY: Orbis, 1978. *"The reforms spawned by Vatican II...": Lernoux, *People of God*, introduction. *Knights of Malta, Vernon Walters: ibid. p. 59. Also Lernoux's chapter on "The Religious International" documents the widespread participation of many of the most powerful people within the capitalist class in the U.S. and abroad in the political/financial dealings of the Knights, especially J. Peter Grace, Jr. the head of the U.S. eastern branch; two directors of the CIA, William Casey under Reagan and John McCone under Kennedy, were Knights, as is conservative ideologue William F. Buckley. (There are perhaps 1,500 Knights in the U.S.(15,000 worldwide) not all of them involved in right-wing anti-communist politics (many rich members, says Lernoux, just like to dress up in fancy costumes, etc.) *"Silencio!...": Conor Cruise O'Brien, "God and Man in Nicaragua."

Chapter 11, COUP DE GRACE: FUNDAMENTALIST AMERICANISM, AN EVANGELICAL COUNTER-REFORMATION (pages 45-50)

*"He is putting down...": Lernoux, *People of God*, p. 158. *"Project Light," Spring of 1990: the author was in Guatemala the week before Robertson's arrival and spoke with a number of evangelicals who were enthusiastic about "Project Light." Volunteers were manning 40 telephones around the clock in downtown Guatemala City (next to the aptly named Sheraton "Conquistador" Hotel which was also the home of Jimmy Swaggart's Guatemalan organization) to answer the calls of those who responded to the TV broadcasts and other forms of advertising; they reported many instant conversions and testimonies of faith taking place over the phone. *percentage of evangelicals: David Martin, *Tongues of Fire: the Explosion of Protestantism in Latin America*, Oxford: Basil Blackwell, 1990, pp. 50-51. David Stoll has estimates in his *Is Latin America Turning Protestant?*, (Berkeley: University of California Press, 1990) based on various studies which may have been more accurate; his numbers are slightly lower but also a little out of date already (most recent from 1986), given the speedy growth of the the evangelicals in all of these countries. Therefore Martin's figures seem reasonable. *Religious Right: Sara Diamond, author of *Spiritual Warfare*, Boston: South End Press, 1989, has done extensive research on the ties and finances that bind right-wing political groups and fundamentalist religion all over the world. *"discipline": the author and Susan D. Rose visited several Verbo services in 1987 and also spent considerable time with the teachers and administrators of their Christian school. (see Rose and Brouwer, "The Export of Fundamentalist Americanism: Evangelical Education in Guatemala," *Latin American Perspectives*, vol. 17, number 4, fall 1990.) The emphasis on "discipline" in evangelical Guatemala evoked memories of Calvin's prescriptions for the rising middle

class merchants in Geneva 400 years ago - R.D. Tawney said (in *Religion and the Rise of Capitalism*): "Discipline Calvin himself described as the nerves of religion." However, the Verbo education in Guatemala, like that of the New Christian Right in the U.S., lacks much of the instinct for humanistic inquiry that characterized early Protestant scholars and theologians and the fledgling capitalists who followed them; the Verbo school is based on arcane concepts drawn from ultra-rightwing writings from the McCarthy era in the U.S. and is intent on constantly warning its students of the diabolical intrusions of secular humanism (one teacher from the U.S. was intent on demonstrating that Dick and Jane reading books were one of these threats.) Early Protestantism, in its relationship to early capitalism, seemed almost revolutionary, providing inspiration to those independent souls who were willing to work and think about a different kind of world, thus replacing the old social structures with a fresh one. Some (Peter Berger and company) are trying to argue that such may be the case today as Protestantism grows in many industrializing societies; however, we see a different kind of Protestantism, one produced under industrial and monopoly capitalism in the North (the U.S.) which is useful for the promotion and spread of transnational corporate capitalism in the South - thus it has less to do with encouraging the spirit of individuals in the Weberian sense, and more to do with controlling the behavior of large groups within intellectually narrow limits so they do not question the mature capitalist system. Paul Gifford has written a very insightful book, *The Religious Right in Southern Africa*, (Harare: Baobab, 1988), which details the activities of U.S.-generated churches in South Africa and Zimbabwe; his analysis of their social and political-economic function is very similar to the one expressed here. *"Second Protestant Internationale": from Peter Berger's forward to David Martin, *Tongues of Fire*, p. viii. *Protestant "explosion": ibid. Martin rightly sees the spread of Protestantism as accompanying the spread of industrialization and the disintegration of old cultures as U.S. culture reigns supreme; however, he seems to offer too much hope that the new religious wave will somehow foster the same kinds of voluntarism and democratic sensibility that grew out of English Puritanism and other 16th, 17th, and 18th century dissenting traditions. He does not seem to give enough attention to the reactionary fundamentalist belief system that is a particular manifestation of 20th century monopoly capitalism; this peculiar theology from the U.S. contains extreme right-wing political attributes. Of course, it is possible that this Protestantism will be transformed into something new and democratic in Latin America by social forces we do not adequately comprehend; however, this would not occur because of its U.S. cultural roots, but in spite of them. *Early Methodism: Robert F. Wearmouth, *Methodism and the Working Class Movement of England*, London: Epworth Press, 1937, and E.P. Thompson, *The Making of the English Working Class*. It is not the intention of the author to demean the history of the Methodists, but merely to point out the similarities between the fast growing "enthusiastic" religions of 200 years ago and those which are spreading around the world today. Present day Methodism is different than at its inception and is now a liberal "mainstream" faith (in which some ministers are even gravitating toward liberation theology.) *"practical Christianity": Wearmouth, p. 140. *"They fostered within...": Thompson, p. 355 *"Hugh Bourne, a humble

carpenter...": Wearmouth, p. 3-5. *"There is a class...": ibid. p. 189. *"men of character": ibid. p. 184 *"the proverbial Non-conformist mill owners": Thompson, p.346.

PART III
Chapter 12, CAPITALIST DEVELOPMENT (pages 51-54)

*"the overwhelming proportion..": Immanuel Wallerstein, *Historical Capitalism*, London: Verso, 1983, p. 101. *"In the 1790s the great landlords...": Eric Wolf, *Europe and the People Without History*, Berkeley: University of California Press, 1982, p. 269. *"In 1844 in Liverpool...": Wearmouth, *Methodism and the Working Class Movement of England*, p. 202. *1842 Parliament's Report: ibid. p. 181. *the job of "hurrying": ibid. p. 182. *"The greater human immiseration...": Wallerstein, p. 104.

Chapter 13, NOT THE LAND OF THE FREE, NOT THE HOME OF THE BRAVE (pages 55-59)

*"Utmost good faith...": Martin Marty, *Righteous Empire*, New York: Dial Press, 1970, p. 7. *"It was the climax...": Zinn, *A People's History of the United States* p. 289. *"I don't go so far...", Teddy Roosevelt: Marty, p. 12. *North American Indian population: discussed at length in Thorton, *American Indian Holocaust and Survival*; see footnote on indigenous population for Chapter 3. *the beaver trade: Eric Wolf, *Europe and the People Without History*, p. 159-161. *"The fur trade thus...": ibid. 161. *"The developmental problem...": Sidney Mintz, "Slavery and Emergent Capitalisms," in *Slavery in the New World*, ed. by Laura Foner and Eugene Genovese. Englewood Cliffs: Prentice Hall, 1969, p. 33.

*export profits from cotton: Wolf, *Europe and the People Without History*, p. 279. *income of 1000 rich white families, etc..: Zinn, *A People's History...*, p. 231. *Madison earned $237 on every slave: Zinn, p. 32. *slave trade between the Atlantic states and the new plantation areas: Richard Sutch, "The Breeding of Slaves for Sale and the Western Expansion of Slavery, 1850-1860," in *Race and Slavery in the Western Hemisphere*, ed. by Eugene Genovese, Princeton: Princeton University Press, 1975. *Discussion of slave life and their treatment in Genovese's *In Red and Black*, Knoxville: University of Tennessee Press, 1984. *last years of slavery in the Caribbean: B.W. Higman, *Slave Populations of the British Caribbean, 1807-1834*, Baltimore: Johns Hopkins, 1984. *The Methodist Church and slavery: Carter Godwin Woodson, *The Negro in Our History*, p. 226.

Chapter 14, U.S. INDUSTRIALIZATION - NOT A PICNIC (pages 60-63)

*strikes in 1835 and 1860: Zinn, *A People's History...*, pp.224-226. *"With the deadliest weapons...": Ibid, p. 349. * Flowerdew Hundred: *Commerce and Conflict: The English in Virginia, 1625*, a pamphlet published by the National Museum of National History, Smithsonian, Washington D.C., for an exhibit mounted from April 1988 to May 1989. pp. 8-9. *white European immigrants to the U.S.: their numbers were huge, and their lack of citizenship (or their second class citizenship) helps explain why it took a while for the industrial unions to take form; Gavin Wright, "The Origins of American

Industrial Success 1879–1940," *American Economic Review*, Sept. 1990. *Anthony Wallace, *Rockdale*, New York: Knopf, 1978. *Sitdown strikes: Zinn, *A People's History*, p. 391. *16% of U.S. workers are organized: *Economic Notes*, March-April 1991, p. 14.

Chapter 15, NEW WAYS OF EXPLOITING AMERICA IN THE 19TH AND 20TH CENTURIES (pages 64–68)

*Chilean income and exports in 1890: Galeano, *Open Veins of Latin America*, p.156-7. *1901 Cuba: Zinn, *A People's History*, p. 303. *1911 Mexico: James Cockcroft, "Social and Economic Structure of the Porfiriato," in *Dependence and Underdevelopment* by Cockcroft, Andre Gunder Frank, and Dale F. Johnson. New York: Doubleday, 1972, p. 62. *British economic control of Cuba: Galeano, *Open Veins*, p. 80. *unwritten agreement backed up by Monroe Doctrine: Williams, *History of the Caribbean*, p. 415. Cuba was the primary concern of President Monroe, who like other North Americans, saw that it would eventually fall into the hands of the U.S. if the British would enter into a "gentlemen's agreement" to leave it in Spanish hands for the time being. Williams quotes Monroe's Secretary of State, John Quincy Adams, who anticipated the events at the end of the 19th century in a letter to the U.S. Minister to Spain in 1823: "There are laws of political as well as physical gravitation... Cuba, forcibly disjoined from its unnatural connection with Spain... can gravitate only toward the North American Union." *1894 cane production: Williams, p. 377. *Roosevelt: "I should welcome almost any war...": Zinn, *A People's History...*, p. 290. *"The island of Cuba...": ibid. p. 291. *In 1958, U.S. sugar: Williams, *History of the Caribbean*, p. 480. *only 4% of the peasantry...: ibid. p. 479. *land in Morelos, and Mexican heads of family, etc.: Cockcroft, *Dependence and Underdevelopment*, pp. 62 and 66. *"On Yucatan henequen plantations...": Galeano, *Open Veins*, p.135. *John Kenneth Turner, *Barbarous Mexico*, Austin: University of Texas, 1969. "The United States has virtually reduced Diaz to a political dependency, and by so doing has virtually transformed Mexico into a slave colony of the United States." *percentage of Mexican exports: Cockcroft, p. 62. *"Consular bourgeoisie": Rudolfo Stavenhagen; the Mexican scholar wrote in the first issue of *Latin American Perspectives* (Spring 1974, volume 1, number 1, p. 135): "if the control of key sectors of the economy has passed into foreign hands; if the rates of investment tend to decrease; if the loss of capital tends to increase; if the levels of the great majority of the population tend to worsen, it is because the ruling classes of Latin American countries have not only been incapable of reversing these tendencies, but on the contrary, have been their principal promoters and beneficiaries..." (that is, they form a "consular bourgeoisie.") This is in contrast with the idea of a national bourgeoisie which theoretically (from a more conventional Marxist point of view) could build up local capitalism to the point where a socialist transformation would be possible. Stavenhagen rejected that idea on the evidence of the Mexican example and sided, more or less, with the "dependency and underdevelopment" side of the argument (a new and incomplete set of ideas challenging Marxist orthodoxy) which saw the developing countries actually being "underdeveloped" (or super-exploited) by their ties to the center of the capitalist world system. This author feels that the dependency theorists have been partially justified by the course of world events, which has seen most countries compelled to subject themselves

to the whims and plans of international capital; the few that have developed successful capitalist institutions of their own (Korea, Taiwan) have done so under very unusual circumstances and without developing the democratic institutions that "national bourgeois" culture was supposed to bring with it (see chapter 18.) This points out one of the constant problems that confronts Marxists and radicals in general: wanting the "revolutionary process" to succeed, they can fall prey to a more optimistic appraisal than social and political realities permit. In this case, the "dependency" theorists were scorned for being too pessimistic about the "people's" ability to create socialism; certainly after the 1970s and 1980s, it looks like the "dependency" view of general capitalist development was substantially correct. Andre Gunter Frank rather accurately predicted that the outcome of the capitalist crisis of the 1980s would be grim for the developing world: "Capitalism itself is undergoing another crisis-generated transition or transformation, of which the relinking of the socialist economies and the analogous reorganization of the Third World to participate in a new international division of labor through so-called export-led growth are integral elements" (*Theories of Development*, Beverly Hills: Sage, 1983); in order to accomplish this transformation, coercion was necessary: "To provide these low wages and indeed to reduce wages from one country to another competitively, as each tries to offer more favorable conditions to international capital, requires political repression, the destruction of labor unions and/or the prohibition of strikes and other union activity, the systematic imprisonment, torture, or assassination of labor and other political leaders and in general the imposition of emergency rule, martial law, and military government." (*Crisis in the World Economy*, London: Heinemann, 1980.). *Mexican Capital Flight: Victor M. Bernal Sahagrin, "The Foreign Debt and Beyond: Alternatives to the Latin American Economic Crisis," *Latin American Perspectives*, winter 1989, vol. 16, no. 1, p. 111–126. He also points out that during roughly the same period, 1982 to 1988, wages dropped by 50%. *The Nitrate War: Galeano, *Open Veins*, p. 156. *3/4 of Chilean exports go through Britain: ibid. *Anaconda and Kennecott - ibid. p. 161. *The story of the food processing factory told to the author by Jose Villa, who worked in the factory and took part in its various political and social activities as well as in the MIR, the Movement of the Revolutionary Left. Jose Villa was rounded up by Pinochet's soldiers, imprisoned, and tortured; finally he was released, sought refuge in a foreign embassy in Santiago, and found asylum in the U.S. where he worked with the author in a worker-owned construction company.

Chapter 16, AMERICAN FREEDOM MEANS THE FREEDOM TO INVEST (pages 69–71)

*flow of investment: *Dependence and Underdevelopment*, p. 379. *profits of top 12 banks: *NACLA Report on the Americas*, July/August 1978, p. 15. *debt of Brazil and Mexico: *World Development Report* of the World Bank, 1989. *"I will tell you...", Luis Da Silva: Arthur McEwan, *Debt and Disorder*, New York: Monthly Review Press, 1990, p. 24. *Collor's access to TV: Donald Ramos, "Elections in Brazil: A Victory for More fo the Same," *Democratic Left*, March/April 1990, p. 15. *"the new emerging world model": Alexander Cockburn, "Ashes and Diamonds," *In These Times*, p. 17, May 1, 1990. *Bush reaction to Brazilian austerity: James

Brooke, "U.S. is Pleased," New York Times, April, 12, 1990. *Generals, repression, growth in public debt, and decline in public spending and decline in workers' wages: *NACLA Report on the Americas*, Nov./Dec. 1989, p. 37. *Mexican and Brazilian auto industries: Rhys Jenkins, *Transnational Corporations and the Latin American Automobile Industry*, Pittsburgh: University of Pittsburgh Press, 1987, p. 222. *auto trade balance: Steve Brouwer, *Sharing the Pie*, Carlisle: Big Picture Books, 1992. *declining U.S. wages: ibid. *"will experience stagnation...": Volker Bornschier and Chirstopher Chase-Dunn, *Transnational Corporations and Underdevelopment*, New York: Praeger, 1985. p. 29–30.

Chapter 17, EXPLOITING THE LAST FRONTIER - THE AMAZON RAINFOREST (pages 72-75)

*best discussion of Brazilian rainforest: Susanna Hecht and Alexander Cockburn, *The Fate of the Forest*, London: Verso, 1990; also see Barbara Weinstein, *The Amazon Rubber Boom*, Palo Alto: Stanford University Press, 1983. *General reading on "Food and Development," one of the important areas (and there are many) which does not get enough attention in this book: the Institute for Food and Development Policy, headed by Francis Moore Lappé and Joseph Collins, produces a number of very valuable books and pamphlets, *Food First Action Alert Bulletins*); Henry Bernstein, Ben Crow, Maureen MacIntosh, *The Food Question: Profits vs. People*, New York: Monthly Review Press, 1990; In the last book mentioned, Harriet Friedman ("The Origins of Third World Food Dependency,") neatly describes major factors of the world food problem: "the history of agriculture in international capitalism is one of the impoverishment of the direct producers, though to different degrees and in different ways, and the degradation of the natural resources which are our common heritage"; and "third world export production is undertaken by agro-capitalists precisely because land and labour are valued so low." *Columbus: see Chapter 1 notes. *1903, the Congo: B. Inglis, *Roger Casement*, London: Hodden and Stoughten, 1973. p. 38. Also see Mark Twain, *King Leopold's Soliloquy*, for anti-imperialist remarks at the beginning of the 20th century. *1912, Peru: Susanna Hecht and Alexander Cockburn, *Fate of the Forest*, p. 20. *"In the Amazon...": "Murder at the Margins of the World," *NACLA Report on the Americas*, May 1989, p. 36. *exploitative agriculture and ownership: Sandra Steingraber and Judith Hurley List, "Brazil's Debt and Deforestation - A Global Warning," *Food First Action Alert*, San Francisco: Institute for Food and Development Policy, 1990. p. 2. *23 of 28 owners: *Fate of the Forest*, p. 146 *land in Acre: ibid. p. 125. *fiscal incentives for beef: ibid. p. 149. *2/3 of Brazilians do not get enough to eat: Steingraber and List, p. 2. *workers incomes decline: *Fate of the Forest*, p. 4. *"inundate the Amazon...": ibid. p. 103. *"A country that hath yet her maidenhead...": quoted in Williams, *History of the Caribbean*, p. 79. *food productivity on small farms: Steingraber and List, p. 2.

PART IV, NORTH VERSUS SOUTH

Chapter 18, SOUTH KOREA - THE DEVELOPMENT MODEL (pages 78-83)

*May, 1980, Kwangju: *The Kwangju Uprising*, ed. Donald N. Clark; Boulder: Westview, 1988. Clark gives the figure of 2,000 dead and missing that is widely accepted among the people of the city (p. 5); the army claims only 200 were killed. In the nationwide repression that followed, 37,000 journalists and teachers were sent to military re-education camps. The Korean struggle for democracy (as opposed to the Korean business news) is woefully underreported in the West, and serious analysis of the Korean political economy has been lacking, too. Two recent books worth looking at: Hak Kyu Sohn, *Authoritarianism and Opposition in South Korea*, London: Routledge, 1989; and Christian Institute for the Study of Justice and Development, *Lost Victory*, Seoul: Minjungsa, 1988. *strikes and riot police: "Workers in Korea Battle Riot Police," *The New York Times*, May 1, 1990. *wages and workers' safety: Pharis Harvey, "No Justice for Workers in Korea," *Democratic Left*, Sept./Oct. 1988, p. 9. *"The girls of Taiwan..": Thorton Bradshaw, chairman of RCA, gave the commencement address to students at Dickinson College in Carlisle, Pennsylvania in May of 1986 and gave a rosy account of the way transnational corporations are spreading North American values and culture. He even mentioned the "girls of Lawrence, Massachusetts" in the 19th century, as if to suggest that they had enjoyed a nice time at work in the early American textile mills.) *Kusadae: Harvey, p. 10. *"to put it in the simplest terms": Mark Clifford, "Seoul-Mates Again," *Far Eastern Economic Review*, Mar. 1, 1990, p. 49. *100 largest U.S. corporations: Steve Brouwer, *Sharing the Pie*, Carlisle: Big Picture Books, 1992. *10 largest Korean corporations: Hang Yul Rhee, "The Economic Problems of the Korean Political Economy," *Political Change in South Korea*, ed. by Kim and Kihl. New York: Paragon House, 1988. p. 207. *the 4 largest chaebol: Clifford, p. 46. *Daewoo production for GM: Lester Thurow, quoted in "The Man with All the Answers," by Charles C. Mann, *The Atlantic Monthly*, January 1990. *Korean egalitarianism: Hang Yul Rhee, op. cit.," p. 195. *some sort of fascism: Charles Barone and Gordon Bergsten, in their as yet unpublished teaching guide for *Radical Political Economy* (Department of Economics, Dickinson College) give a nice concise definition of the worldwide phenomenon (which obviously doesn't openly call itself Fascist, like Mussolini's Party of the 1920s and 30s): "Fascism used in Nazi Germany and Mussolini's Italy and the similar authoritarianism used in many Third World countries today, is a political/military response to class conflict that suspends political democracy, represses opposition political parties, and outlaws independent working class organizations in favor of high profits and conditions favorable to capitalists. Fascism is thus used to limit workers' demands." *"500,000 Church members" and "it seems like the ancient practice known as 'sheep stealing'": David Martin, *Tongues of Fire*, p. 143. *"a Korean messiah...": Frank Greve, "Moon Mixes God, Money, and Politics," *The Philadelphia Inquirer*, Dec. 20, 1987, p. 1 and 18. *"Basically trying to take over...": quoted by Tom Barry, Deb Preusch, and Beth Sims, *The New Right Humanitarians*, Albuquerque: The Resource Center, 1986., p. 49. *KCIA, Washington Times, and the Nicaragua Freedom Fund: *New Right Humanitarians* and Greve, p. 18. Greve also comments on the major financial connections between Moon and Richard Viguerie, once the star fund-raiser of the New Right, and Terry Dolan, who headed the National Conservative Political Action Committee; even stranger was the Unification Church's ability to recruit former liberals, like Ralph Abernathy of the SCLC and Eugene McCarthy, to sit on the boards of its subsidiary organizations or chair its academic, religious, and journalistic conferences - these have been held, says Greve, for thousands of "opinion leaders" and "inter-city ministers" at "luxury hotels in Paris, London, Tokyo, Seoul, Los Angeles, and Miami." A Filipino theologian (and a frank exponent of liberation theology) told the author that he was lured into attending a fancy "Moonie"-controlled conference in Japan since its literature did not mention the Unification Church and there were so many impressive scholars taking part. *"to purge...": Moon quoted by Greve, p. 18. *Moon in Moscow, investments in China: Silvia Aloisa, "Setta di potere," *Panorama*, Dec. 2, 1990, p. 98. According to Aliosa, Moon controls more than 15 newspapers around the world, and a great many corporations and banks (10 of the latter are in the tiny country of Uruguay.) *South Africa and *The Washington Times*: Sara Diamond, *Spiritual Warfare: the Politics of the Christian Right*, Boston: South End Press, 1989, p. 195. *CAUSA in the Philippines: Sara Diamond, p. 191. Paul Gifford, in *The Religious Right in Southern Africa*, reveals a great deal about Moonie connections to various right wing religious and political groups there. *Source of Moon's funds: *Frontline*, the in-depth reporting show offered by the Public Broadcasting System, featured the Reverend Moon and his political and financial connections on January 21, 1992. Most of his mysterious billions seem to flow from Japan, where Moon began using his youthful religious converts to support rightwing demonstrations in the 1960s; Moon has close ties with right-wing Japanese businessmen and gangsters, including one aging fascist billionaire who was an admirer of Mussolini and was convicted of war crimes after the Japanese defeat in World War II.

Chapter 19, THE GLOBAL ECONOMY - CAPITALIST VALUES IMPOSED WORLDWIDE (pages 84-89)

*per capita income North and South: *World Development Report*, World Bank, 1989. *"We have seen the development...": Karl Marx, *Capital*, Chapter XXV, Section 3. *Korean economy slows: James Sterngold, "Korea boils as economy cools," *The New York Times*, Business Day, p. 1, May 10, 1990. *Thailand growth: "Out of Primary School," *Far Eastern Economic Review*, July 26, 1990, p. 50 - 52. *Thai auto production and Japanese control: David Singer, "Behind the Thai Boom," *The New York Times*, May 18, 1990, p. 1. *Malaysian exports: "Out of Primary School," p. 52. *Your Majesty...": Judith Todd, *Rhodesia*, Bristol: MacGibbon and Kee Ltd., 1966, p. 17. *"the white man...": ibid. p. 16. *"Private international banking...": Jeff Garth, "U.S. seeks tougher line of flight capital," *The New York Times*, Business Section, Feb. 12, 1990, p. 1. *"Rich investors...": ibid. quoting James S. Henry, economist for bank consulting firm. *"The growth of flight capital...": ibid. *"The moral obligation of commercial intercourse...": quoted by Harry Magdoff, "The American Empire and the U.S. Economy," *Monthly Review*, November 1966.

Chapter 20, NEW WORLD ORDER, SAME OLD EMPIRE (pages 90-93)

*"The world is divided...": Dulles quoted on title page of George Black's *Garrison Guatemala*, London: Zed, 1984. *"The desire and need...": Harry Magdoff, *Imperialism: From the Colonial Age to the Present*, New York: Monthly Review Press, 1978. p. 120. *percentage of earth's land surface controlled by Europe: Magdoff, p.

108. *"As former director of the CIA, Bush...": John Polger in his column in *New Statesman/New Society*, Feb. 1, 1991. *citizens identifying "big oil": this was the impression of the author as he watched three months of CBS Evening News while living in Italy; the U.S. public definitely did not seem keen on war in spite of the incredible propaganda barrage (with very little hard news about Kuwait and Iraq) which CBS was unleashing almost every night; after the war began, of course, everybody started to wave flags and cheer the home team. *"as late as 1972, the seven...": John M. Blair, *The Control of Oil*, New York: Random House, 1978, p. 52. *The Gulf War marks the dawning...": Joshua Muravchik, editorial page, *The New York Times*, quoted by Stephen F. Diamond, "A new deck of playing cards for the nation's anti-war table," *In These Times*, Feb.13-19, 1991, p. 16.

Chapter 21, THE WORLD SYSTEM LOOKS THE SAME (pages 94-96)

- "Humanity is thus faced...": Samir Amin, *Eurocentrism*, New York: Monthly Review, 1989, p. 148.

Chapter 22, SAVING OUR PLANET (pages 97-101)

*Platform of the Brazilian Rubber Tappers' Union: Hecht and Cockburn, *Fate of the Forest*, page 227. *1986 energy use: Lester Brown, et al, *The State of the World*, Worldwatch Report, New York: Norton, 1990. *Sweden: obviously Sweden is not utopia and has its faults and peculiarities; also it is not easy to be the most progressive of European nations in social policy at a time when the rest of the world is being pulled rightward; thus there are economic tensions created by trying to maintain Sweden's very successful record in the international manufacturing market when there is so much competition from industrializing low wage countries and older capitalist countries, like Britain, which are intent on cutting their social programs, crushing union movements, and generally penalizing the bottom 80% of the population. Recent books that discuss Swedish society: Michael Harrington, *Socialism Past and Future*, New York: Little, Brown, 1989; Henry Milner, *Sweden: Social Democracy in Practice*, New York: Oxford University Press, 1989. *Kerala: Richard W. Franke and Barbara H. Chasin, "Kerala State, India: Radical Reform and Development," *Monthly Review*, January 1991, p. 20, and their book, *Kerala: Radical Reform as Development in an Indian State*, San Francisco: Institute for Food and Development Policy, 1989.

Chapter 23, RED AND GREEN (page 102-106)

*"There is something important about women...": *I, Rigoberta Menchu: An Indian Woman in Guatemala*, a testimony edited and introduced by Elisabeth Burgos-Debray, London: Verso, 1984, p. 220. *"It is a radical proposal...": Lula quoted from the introduction he wrote for the Workers' Party presidential platform in 1989, in Maria Helena Moreira Alves, "Building Democratic Socialism: the Partido Dos Trabalhadores in Brazil," *Monthly Review*, Sept. 1990, p. 5.

GENERAL SOURCES AND SUGGESTED READINGS

There are three important works which were indispensible to the author in thinking about how to portray the capitalist conquest as it has taken place throughout the world and its special effects upon the Americas and the United States. The reader is urged to read these books, which go far beyond the limitations of this thin volume:

—Ferdnand Braudel, *Capitalism and Civilization*, New York: Harper and Row, (three volumes: 1981, 1982, 1984) - deals with the emergence of the capitalist system in the 15th to 18th centuries, and also manages to relate these developments to present day worldwide capitalist structures. This lively writing (by one of the most important historians of the 20th century) manages to capture the contradictory nature of capitalism: the energy of everyday trading and productive activity on the one hand; the oppression and inequality imposed by the upper class control over a world political economy, on the other.

—Eduardo Galeano, *Memories of Fire*, New York: Pantheon, 1985, 1987, 1988 - a three volume collection of short and beautifully constructed historical anecdotes, stories, and myths which does nothing less than tell the history of the Americas over the last five hundred years.

—Howard Zinn, *A People's History of the United States*, New York: Harper and Row, 1980 - the history of the U.S. as told from the point of view of the common people, with an emphasis on the pattern of popular resistance to oligarchical rule, racial and sexual oppression, and economic exploitation.

The following books, which generally deal with the spread of the capitalist system and its culture, are also highly recommended:

—Samir Amin, *Eurocentrism*, New York: Monthly Review Press, 1990: a wisely argued critique of the Western presumption of cultural superiority.

—Eric Hobsbawm, *Industry and Empire*, Harmondsworth: Penguin Books, 1969: the industrial revolution and English imperial expansion.

—Harry Magdoff, *The Age of Imperialism*, New York: Monthly Review, 1969: particularly instructive on how the United States assumed the role of enforcing capitalist expansion.

—E.P. Thompson, *The Making of the English Working Class*, New York: Pantheon, 1964: the history and culture produced by the English working class during the first century of the industrial revolution.

—Immanuel Wallerstein, *Historical Capitalism*, London: Verso, 1983: instructive, along with his other books, in defining the "world system" under capitalism.

—Eric R. Wolf, *Europe and the People Without History*, Berkeley: University of California Press, 1982: an anthropologist's account of the history of most of the world's people as they encountered European and capitalist expansion.

FURTHER READING

Barnet, Richard, and Muller, Ronald, *Global Reach*, New York: Simon and Schuster, 1974.

Barry, Tom, *Roots of Rebellion: Land and Hunger in Central America*, Boston: South End Press, 1987. _____ and Preusch, Deb, *The Central American Fact Book*, New York: Grove Press, 1986.

Michel Beaud, *A History of Capitalism, 1500-1980*, New York: Monthly Review Press, 1983.

Bernstein, Henry, Ben Crow, and Maureen MacIntosh, *The Food Question: Profits vs. People*, New York: Monthly Review Press, 1990.

Berryman, Philip, *The Religious Roots of Rebellion*, Maryknoll, NY: Orbis Press, 1984.

Black, George, *Good Neighbors*, New York: Pantheon, 1989.

Bornschier, Volker, and Chase-Dunn, Christopher, *Transnational Corporations and Underdevelopment*, New York: Praeger, 1985.

Brouwer, Steve, *Sharing the Pie*, Carlisle: Big Picture Books, 1992.

Brown, Lester, et al, *The State of the World*, a Worldwatch Report, New York: Norton, 1990.

Cockcroft, James, Andre Gunter Frank, and Dale F. Johnson, *Dependence and Underdevelopment*, New York: Doubleday, 1972.

Davidson, Basil, *The African Slave Trade*, Boston: Little Brown, 1961.

de las Casas, Bartolome, *History of the Indies*, New York: Harper and Row, 1971.

Diamond, Sara, *Spiritual Warfare: The Politics of the Christian Right*, Boston: South End Press, 1989.

Foner, Laura, and Genovese, Eugene, *Slavery in the New World*, Englewood Cliffs, NJ: Prentice Hall, 1969.

Frank, Andre Gunter, *World Accumulation, 1492-1789*, New York: Monthly Review Press, 1978.

Franke, Richard W., and Chasin, Barbara H., *Kerala: Radical Reform as Development in an Indian State*, San Francisco: Institute for Food and Development Policy, 1989.

Furtado, Celso, *Economic Development of Latin America: Historical Background and Contemporary Problems*, New York: Cambridge University Press, 1976.

Galeano, Eduardo, *Open Veins of Latin America*, New York: Monthly Review Press, 1973.

Gifford, Paul, *The Religious Right in Southern Africa*, Harare: Baobab, 1988.

Granzotto, Gianni, *Christopher Columbus*, New York: Doubleday, 1985.

Gutman, Herbert, *Work, Culture, and Society in Industrializing America*, New York: Random House, 1977.

Hak Kyu Sohn, *Authoritarianism and Opposition in South Korea*, London: Routledge, 1989.

Handy, Jim, *Gift of the Devil*, Boston: South End Press, 1984.

Hecht, Susanna, and Cockburn, Alexander, *The Fate of the Forest*, London: Verso, 1990.

Kolko, Joyce, *Restructuring the World Economy*, New York: Pantheon, 1988.

Lernoux, Penny, *People of God*, New York: Viking, 1989.

MacEwan, Arthur, *Debt and Disorder: International Economic Instability and U.S. Imperial Decline*, New York: Monthly Review Press, 1990.

Magdoff, Harry, *Imperialism: from the Colonial Age to the Present*, New York: Monthly Review Press, 1978.

Mandel, Ernest, *The Second Slump*, London: Verso, 1980.

Martin, David, *Tongues of Fire: the Explosion of Protestantism in Latin America*, Oxford: Basil Blackwell, 1990.

Marty, Martin, *Righteous Empire*, New York: Dial Press, 1970.

Marx, Karl, *Capital* vols. I-III, New York: International Publishers, 1967.

Menchu, Rigoberta, *I, Rigoberta Menchu: an Indian Woman in Guatemala*, London: Verso, 1984.

Milner, Henry, *Sweden: Social Democracy in Practice*, New York: Oxford University Press, 1989.

Sale, Kirkpatrick, *The Conquest of Paradise*, New York: Knopf, 1990.

Schlesinger, Stephen, and Kinzer, Stephen, *Bitter Fruit*, New York: Doubleday, 1981.

Thorton, Russell, *American Indian Holocaust and Survival*, Norman: University of Oklahoma Press, 1987.

Wallace, Anthony, *Rockdale*, New York: Knopf, 1978.

Wearmouth, Robert F., *Methodism and the Working Class Movement of England*, London: Epworth Press, 1937.

Williams, Eric, *The History of the Caribbean: From Columbus to Castro*, New York: Harper and Row, 1971.

Woodson, Carter Godwin, *The Negro in Our History*, Washington: Associated Publishers, 1922.

PERIODICALS AND NEWSPAPERS

Business Week
Far Eastern Economic Review
In These Times
Latin American Perspectives
The Manchester Guardian
Monthly Review
New Statesman/New Society
NACLA Report on the Americas
The New York Times
The Wall Street Journal

THANKS to my wife, Susan, who is both tolerant and supportive of my efforts to make political economy and social issues comprehensible to the general reader.

And thanks to working people in the Americas and the rest of the world, who generally work hard and skillfully and receive too little in return. We live on a richly endowed planet which offers all of us the possibility of earning a living, raising families, enhancing the quality of our communities, and otherwise enjoying the beauty and diversity of life on earth. If we can learn to share with each other, the future should be brighter for all nations, North and South.

- Steve Brouwer, January 1992

ABOUT THE AUTHOR

Steve Brouwer, the author and illustrator of this book, writes frequently on economics, politics, and American culture. With his wife, sociologist Susan Rose, he has written scholarly articles and academic papers in political science, education, and sociology. By trade a carpenter and designer of houses, he has also engaged in a number of successful business enterprises that practice democratic economics: these include cooperatives, a worker-owned construction company, and a community-owned rental housing program. Steve Brouwer is the father of four, two in college and two in diapers, and lives with his family in a cabin in the woods of Southern Pennsylvania.